Getting the most out of your
RADIAL SAW

Rockwell Handbooks

Getting the most out of your
RADIAL SAW

WITH A SPECIAL CHAPTER ON THE MOTORIZED MITER BOX

a Rockwell Publication

A complete handbook describing the radial saw and the motorized miter box in the home workshop with more than three hundred photographic illustrations and line drawings.

Rockwell International

Tool Group
400 North Lexington Avenue
Pittsburgh, Pennsylvania 15208

Foreword

"Getting The Most Out Of Your Radial Saw" is published as a service to power tool users. Because different makes, models, and sizes of machines vary in their performance and features, the editors have tried to make the information in this handbook as general as possible.

The radial saw is one of the most basic and useful tools to be found in the home workshop. It is also one of the safest. But, as with any power tool, certain safety precautions must be followed. These procedures are included throughout the book and are detailed in Chapter 2.

Radial saws are available in several sizes and two basic designs. When selecting a machine, make sure it will meet your requirements. If you intend to use your radial saw for long, sustained periods of time, you should consider buying a unit with a greater capacity and heavier duty construction. Also, be certain that the machine you select can be adapted for all of the operations you will perform on it.

This book was designed to accommodate both the beginner, wanting to learn the basic operations of the radial saw, and the skilled artisan needing information about a single more complex, area of sawing or one of the other applications of this valuable tool.

Originally published in 1969, this handbook has been reprinted several times, and has evolved into both a compendium and a final word about radial saws. This most recent edition includes all applicable information from the previous edition, as well as the latest in available woodworking techniques. This edition also has a separate chapter on the motorized miter box. Material for this book was based on information gathered from sources throughout the power tool industry. It is the greatest hope and desire of the editors that you will "get the most out of your radial saw," after reading this book.

Rockwell International
Tool Group

Copyright © 1969 Rockwell Manufacturing Company
Copyright © 1978 Rockwell International Corporation
Published by Rockwell International

Text prepared and book designed by
Robert Scharff & Associates

Library of Congress Catalog Card Number: 78-65523

Manufactured in the United States of America

Contents

Fig. 1-1: A typical 10-inch radial saw.

Chapter 1

GETTING TO KNOW THE RADIAL SAW

If all of the owners of home workshops were told they could only own one stationary power tool, but were given the choice of what it would be, the majority would choose a radial saw. This would be equally true for professional carpenters, shop instructors, and construction workers. Why? No other single piece of shop equipment can perform such a wide range of woodworking operations as efficiently. The basic sawing operations can be performed on the radial saw, as well, if not better, than on any other stationary saw. The value of a power tool is recognized by anyone who has accomplished similar tasks with both hand and power saws. Using a power saw brings an increase in production and a decrease in expended energy.

However, the most valuable asset of the radial saw is its versatility. To call the radial saw a complete workshop in itself would not be much of an exaggeration. There are actually only six basic saw cuts in woodworking: ripping, bevel ripping, crosscutting, bevel crosscutting, mitering, and bevel mitering (all other cuts, no matter how intricate, are combinations of these basic cuts). The radial saw makes all of these cuts equally well. And, with accessories and attachments, the radial saw can be quickly and simply made to function as a jointer, boring machine, router, sander (disk and drum), buffer and polisher, and can easily perform shaping, molding, and dadoing operations, as well.

SIZES AND CONSTRUCTION

Radial saw sizes are determined by the largest diameter blade the saw can accommodate. A 10-inch model, for example, uses a 10-inch diameter saw blade. The most widely used saws in the home shop and light construction trades are the 10- and 12-inch models. Saw capacity is determined approximately by blade size. For example, a 10-inch model will cut wood to a 3-inch depth; a 12-inch model will cut to a 4-inch depth. Other common sizes include the 14-inch, 16-inch, and 18-inch saws. These larger sizes are used chiefly in industry and the building and lumber trades. (*Note:* All dimensions in this book are given in English measurements. A chart for metric conversions is on page 120. Incidentally, the rip scales on some radial saws feature a metric scale.)

The operation of the radial saw (Fig. 1-1) is fairly simple. Most are equipped with a direct-drive motor. These have no belts, pulleys, gears or other devices to maintain or worry about. The cutting tool is mounted directly on the motor spindle, an operation done above the worktable so that there are no table inserts to deal with. With most machines, the direct-drive motor has sealed-for-life bearings at each end of the motor shaft.

Motors of this type are usually equipped with a manual-reset overload relay button which kicks out when the motor is overloaded. If the motor shuts off or fails to start because of overheating, overloading, or inadequate voltage, turn the switch to the "off"position, let the motor cool for three to five minutes, and push the reset button, which will reset the overload device. If you do not hear a "click" when the button is pressed, allow the motor to cool a little longer. When the "click" is heard, the motor can be turned on again in the usual

1

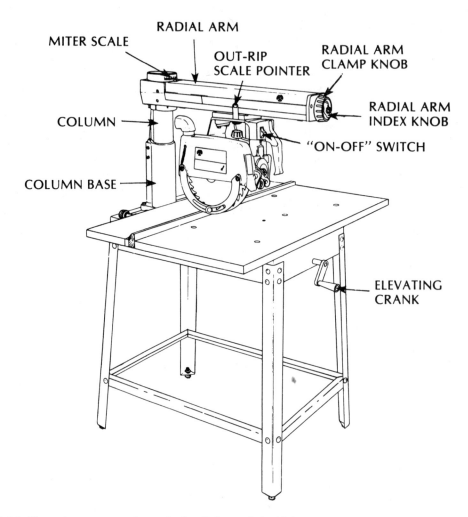

MITER SCALE

RADIAL ARM

OUT-RIP
SCALE POINTER

RADIAL ARM
CLAMP KNOB

COLUMN

RADIAL ARM
INDEX KNOB

COLUMN BASE

"ON-OFF" SWITCH

ELEVATING
CRANK

Fig. 1-2A: The primary parts of a typical radial saw (left side).

manner. Of course, any voltage problems should be corrected.

Many radial saws are also equipped with a brake which automatically stops the blade within a few seconds after turning off the saw or when power is lost.

Principle of Operation. The radial saw (Figs. 1-2A and B) is in effect a mechanical arm that duplicates the dexterity of a human arm. It can make all movements with controlled accuracy in every operation. When cutting lumber, for instance, the human element makes it impossible for even an expert carpenter to cut two boards

exactly alike; but the mechanical arm, with its ballbearing carriage riding on precision-machined tracks, guarantees accuracy on every cut. Accuracy and safety are further ensured, because all cutting is done from the top of the work material, and the operator can see exactly what is happening.

The cutting tool on the radial saw can be placed in any position in all three dimensions (length, width, and depth). The design, allowing full maneuverability in any of three directions, makes this possible. The *travel* or *radial arm* can be rotated 360 degrees around a *column*, but automat-

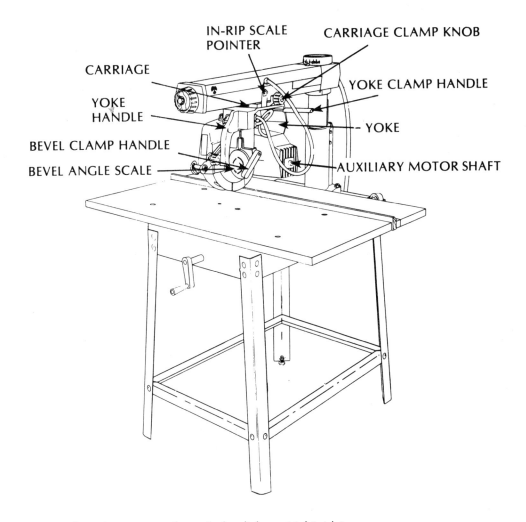

IN-RIP SCALE POINTER

CARRIAGE CLAMP KNOB

CARRIAGE

YOKE CLAMP HANDLE

YOKE HANDLE

YOKE

BEVEL CLAMP HANDLE

BEVEL ANGLE SCALE

AUXILIARY MOTOR SHAFT

Fig. 1-2B: The primary parts of a typical radial saw (right side).

ically locks (indexes) at 0 degrees, 45 degrees left, and 45 degrees right, unless the "built-in" radial arm *index knob* is released. In any position—even one of the "lock" positions—the arm must be locked with the *radial arm clamp knob* to secure it.

On the typical radial saw, an eye-level calibrated *miter scale* at the top of the column, with a pointer attached near the back of the arm, indicates the arm setting at any position from 0 degrees to 90 degrees, right or left. The wood for miter cuts never has to be shifted; the travel arm puts the saw at the exact angle wanted. The blade is simply pulled across the wood to make the cut.

The cutting tool and motor are held by a *yoke*, which can be swiveled 360 degrees on a *carriage*, which in turn moves along the arm. The yoke on some radial saws has as many as six "index" positions: 0 degrees (when the blade is aligned with the arm and facing the operator), 45 degrees and 90 degrees right, 45 and 90 degrees left, and 180 degrees (when the blade is aligned with the arm, but facing away from the front of the saw); others lock only at the four 90-degree positions, to give quick ad-

3

justment for ripping and crosscutting. A *yoke clamp handle* locks the cuttinghead (motor and blade) in the desired position. The yoke must be clamped to eliminate play in every position—even the "index" positions.

The carriage can be moved manually to any desired position along the arm. Usually, there is a *scale* on each side of the arm: one indicates the *"out-ripping"* position, the other, the *"in-ripping"* position. A *carriage clamp knob* must be tightened to lock the carriage to the arm. However, this knob should be left loose, if an operation requires moving the carriage—and the cuttinghead with it—along the arm. **Never leave the carriage unclamped when the motor is running**, unless you are holding the *yoke handle.*

The blade and motor can also be manually tilted in the yoke 180 degrees in either direction. However, the amount of tilt is limited by the blade guard or by any accessory mounted at either end of the motor shaft. Most radial saws have five automatic "index" positions: (1) with the *auxiliary motor shaft* at 90 degrees (vertical and at the bottom); (2) with the auxiliary shaft at 45 degrees; (3) with both the auxiliary and the primary motor shaft at 0 degrees (horizontal—putting the saw blade in a vertical position); (4) with the primary shaft at 45 degrees; and (5) with the primary shaft at 90 degrees (vertical, at the bottom, putting the saw blade in a horizontal position). The first two positions can only be reached with the saw blade and the blade guard on the primary shaft removed. The last two positions can be obtained only when nothing is mounted on the auxiliary motor shaft. At any angle tilt position, including the "index" positions, the blade and motor must be locked into place with the *bevel clamp handle* to eliminate play. A *scale and pointer* on the yoke, behind the yoke handle, indicates in degrees the blade bevel-angle setting. Compound angles (bevel miters) and bevel cuts are measured for you with accuracy, with no limit to the

Fig. 1-3: Swinging the arm horizontally around the column.

number of bevel cuts.

Finally, the typical radial saw has an *elevating crank* which moves the column vertically in the *column base*, to raise and lower the arm, and the cuttinghead with it, to the desired depth of cut on any particular workpiece. Each full turn generally raises or lowers the cutting tool 1/8 inch, each half turn 1/16 inch.

When using a radial saw, you have to remember that its flexible operation is based on three simple radial and two slid-

Fig. 1-4: On some radial saw models, the carriage slides on an arm that is pivoted on a fixed overarm.

4

Fig. 1-5: Revolving the yoke 360 degrees under its carriage.

Fig. 1-8: The column holding the arm can be raised or lowered as desired.

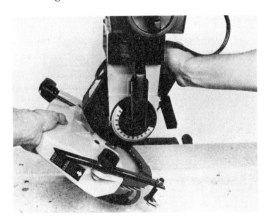

Fig. 1-6: The blade and motor can be tilted within the yoke to any angle desired.

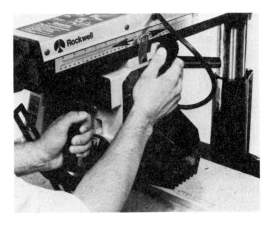

Fig. 1-7: Sliding the carriage back and forth along the arm.

ing adjustments. The arm can be swung horizontally 360 degrees around its column (Fig. 1-3); on some machines the construction is such that the carriage slides on an arm that is pivoted on a fixed overarm (Fig. 1-4); the yoke can be revolved horizontally 360 degrees under its carriage (Fig. 1-5); and the blade and motor can be tilted within the yoke to any angle desired (Fig. 1-6). Also, the carriage holding the yoke and cuttinghead slides back and forth along the arm (Fig. 1-7), and the column holding the arm can be raised or lowered as desired (Fig. 1-8). These adjustments enable you to easily place the cutting tool in any position.

With so flexible a machine, the average operator will quickly be able to perform many different cuts and other procedures. On the other hand, if an operator is interested in just one operation, the radial saw will perform as efficiently as any single-purpose tool. And, if a change in project design or in work method is necessary, the radial saw can be quickly changed to perform with equal efficiency for another job.

Certainly, another advantage of the radial saw over all other stationary power saws including the table saw, is the simple fact that, except for rip-type operations, the cutting tool and not the workpiece is moved. This makes the radial saw handy for a one-operator shop, where cumbersome

5

workpieces are hard to shift for cutting.

Standard Radial Saw Features. On the radial saw, the cutting tool is guided through the workpiece, or in the case of ripping operations, the workpiece is guided through the saw by means of a *worktable* (Fig. 1-9). The worktable usually consists of four pieces. The larger front table board is in a fixed position, bolted to two steel channels. On some radial saws, the front table board has two table adjusting screws; one pulls the center of the table down if it is bowed up; the other raises the center if it is bowed down. For standard cutting operations, a table fence is located next to the front table board. It acts as a back stop for crosscutting and as a guide edge for ripping. Behind the table fence are a spacer board and a rear board. The table fence, spacer board, and rear board are all movable and can be arranged to suit the operation and size and shape of the workpiece (Fig. 1-10). The interchangeable table boards and table fence lie on steel channels and are held in place by two table-board clamps which wedge them in behind the stationary front table. When the radial saw is positioned for edge molding while feeding along the fence, the molding cutter cannot be lowered to table-top level unless there is a cut-out in the rear table board into which the arbor end can be lowered.

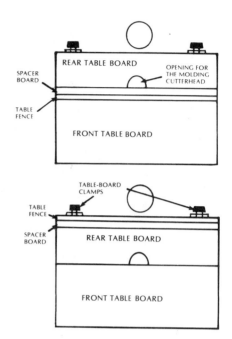

Fig. 1-10: The table fence, spacer board, and rear table board can be arranged as needed for each job.

Radial saws may be built into a workbench, placed on a steel or wood cabinet, or come with their own accessory legs (Fig. 1-11). For radial saws with legs, caster sets which will increase mobility are available (Fig. 1-12).

If your saw comes without its own legs, it is best to fasten it to a supporting surface using the holes in the bottom flange of the saw base. As a temporary installation and for outdoor construction work, the radial saw can be mounted on saw horses; however, the horses must provide level and steady support. The radial saw can be practically used for outdoor work, because most smaller models are light enough to be easily carried by two average-sized workers.

Protective Devices. A *blade guard* (Fig. 1-13A) fitted with an anti-kickback attachment is standard equipment on all radial saws. The guard is designed to cover the end of the saw arbor for added safety. The blade guard may also be fitted with a retractable *leaf guard* (Fig. 1-13B) covering

Fig. 1-9: A typical radial saw worktable.

Fig. 1-11: Accessory legs for a radial saw.

the sides of the bottom of the cutting tool, to offer the operator lateral protection in normal cutting operations. During ripping or grooving operations, the rear of the blade guard should be tilted down, just clearing the material being cut. This will keep the sawdust from being thrown toward the operator and also prevents the stock from being picked up off the table. The guard may be tilted to any position and securely locked there by means of the *guard clamp knob* (Fig. 1-13C) which holds it to the motor housing. The *anti-kickback fingers* or *pawls* (Fig. 1-13D), as they are also called, ride on the work when ripping, preventing it from bucking or "kicking back" toward the operator. In operation the arm holding the fingers is lowered until the fingers are 1/8 inch below the surface edge of the material. The *splitter* or *spreader* (Fig. 1-13E) is a piece of metal or plastic which helps keep the kerf (saw cut) open. This helps prevent the wood from binding on the blade and causing kick-back. It is especially important to use the splitter for all ripping operations. A *dust spout* (Fig. 1-13F) is usually built into the blade guard to direct sawdust away from the operator and the material being cut.

Power and Speed. Most radial saw

Fig. 1-12: A radial saw with caster sets has increased mobility.

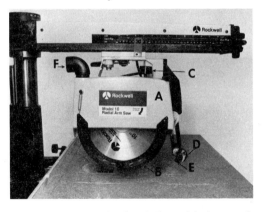

Fig. 1-13: (A) A typical radial saw blade guard; (B) a retractable leaf guard; (C) the blade guard clamp knob; (D) the anti-kickback fingers, also called pawls; (E) the splitter or spreader; and (F) the dust spout.

motors operate at 3450 rpm and are available in either 120-volt single-phase 60-hertz alternating-current, or 240- or 480-volt three-phase 60-hertz alternating-current models. The rated horsepower of radial saw motors ranges from about 1 to 7 1/2 hp, with the 1 1/2 hp being "average" for the home shop.

When it comes to actually cutting the wood, it will be found that the wiring in the shop is as important as the size of the horsepower rating of the motor. In other words, the motor cannot and will not put out any more power than goes into it from the power line. A line that is intended for lights only will not properly carry a power tool motor. Wire that is heavy enough for a short distance may be too light for a greater distance. The line that is adequate for one tool, may have to be replaced when two, three, or more tools plus some lights are to be run on one line. Have an electrician check the line before you go to any expense getting larger and more powerful motors. It may be necessary to have a suitable circuit installed.

What to Look for When Buying a Radial Saw. Radial saws are sold in many different makes and models, each with its own characteristics and features. However, certain general quality and operating features will apply to every model, and it is well for all prospective tool users to study their anticipated purchase for the following items. Here are some points to check when buying a radial saw:

1. The controls should all be conveniently placed within easy reach and they should perform their function in a satisfactory manner. Check especially the on-off switch for the motor, to be sure it is within reach, and that an emergency stop can be made without groping or fumbling. The switch should also be lockable.

2. A wide-spaced, sealed ballbearing roller carriage affords maximum rigidity and accuracy for the life of the saw. Make sure all sliding and pivoting parts move easily for accuracy when cutting.

3. Look for adjustable miter and bevel stops. These will ensure perfect 45 degree and 90 degree bevel and miter cuts.

4. Bevel and miter scales should be large enough to be easily read, and conveniently located to make quick, accurate settings.

5. A brake which automatically stops the blade within a few seconds after the saw is turned off or when the power is lost is a valuable safety feature to consider when buying your saw. Because the direct-drive motors of radial saws are equipped with high-quality ball bearings, the cutting tool on the motor shaft normally continues to revolve for a considerable length of time after the motor is shut off. This drift time ordinarily can vary from 3 to 5 minutes, depending on the size and weight of the tool being used. The efficiency of a brake of this type can be attested to by the fact that it brings the blade to a complete stop in a matter of a few seconds.

6. Look for a sufficiently powerful double shaft motor for cutting heavy material. The second shaft (the other end of the primary shaft) can be equipped with a chuck or adaptor for drum sanding, straight or angle drilling, and routing, after removing any blade, cutter, drum, or disk as well as the blade guard from the primary shaft.

7. The guard should be designed for safety, minimum interference, and maximum visibility. Be sure that the guard includes a splitter and anti-kickback fingers, which add to the safety of the saw and help prevent kickback when ripping.

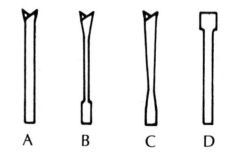

Fig. 1-14: (A) Flatground; (B) thin-rimmed; (C) hollow-ground; and (D) carbide-tipped blades.

8. Look for a table that is smooth, for ease in feeding the work, accuracy, and a good appearance. Make sure the table frame is adequate for the purpose of maintaining accuracy.

9. Be certain you can get proper replacement parts and service, if needed.

10. A complete line of accessories will help you get the most from your machine. Accessories which are supplied by the manufacturer of the tool are designed for the particular machine that you buy, making it unnecessary to use makeshift arrangements to use them to their best advantage.

11. It costs very little more at the start, and much less in the long run to equip your workshop with the best in power tools. Choose a radial saw produced by a manufacturer who has established a record of quality and reliability.

SAW BLADES

While there are many different kinds of radial saw blades, all have one thing in common: They must cut a kerf slightly wider than their body to avoid binding and overheating. This necessary clearance is accomplished in one of three ways:

1. By setting or bending teeth to one side or the other alternately to create added width at the tips. Such blades are called *flatground blades* (Fig. 1-14A) and their kerfs are about 1/8 inch (large teeth) to 3/32 inch (small teeth). The teeth must be kept sharp and properly set or the blade will wander from the cut line and bind. Flat-ground or set-tooth blades are easy to re-sharpen.

2. By grinding or tapering the blade sides to leave the tooth tips wider. If the blade is *thin-rimmed* (Fig. 1-14B), the blade gets its clearance because the material between the teeth and the hub has been ground out leaving the ends of the teeth the original thickness of the blade. On the other hand, the *hollow-ground or taper-rim blade* (Fig. 1-14C) receives its clearance from the fact that the material from the top

of the teeth to the hub is ground in a taper. The hollow-ground blade permits full-depth cuts and makes a kerf of about 3/32 inch. The thin-rimmed blade is limited to the depth of the ground-out section (usually about 1 1/2 inches), but the kerf is usually narrower. Both the hollow-ground and thin-rimmed blades cut smoother than the equivalent flat-ground types. They are both easy to recondition.

3. By brazing on tungsten carbide tooth tips that are slightly wider than the blade, the *carbide-tipped swage blade* (Fig. 1-14D) may be flat-ground (straight across) or beveled in alternate directions. The kerf is about 1/8 inch. While such blades stay sharp longer than other types, they are more expensive in original cost, and if dulled or damaged, the blades must be factory reconditioned.

In addition to the blade type, the sizes and shapes of the blade teeth and gullets determine the kind of work a blade will do. There are several types of common blades (Fig. 1-15).

Crosscut Blade. The crosscut blade is a flat-ground blade designed for cutting across wood grain, giving a fairly smooth cut. Its fine crosscut teeth are set alternately and are filed with a bevel on both the

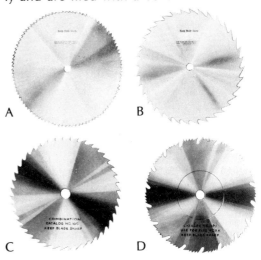

Fig. 1-15: Typical tooth pattern of (A) crosscut; (B) rip; (C) standard combination; and (D) novelty-tooth combination blades.

face and back. The teeth are small in size and filed to a sharp point so that they will sever the wood fibers as they move across the grain. The gullets are small because only a fine sawdust is produced when crosscutting. This blade may also be used for crosscutting plywood, veneer, and various other composition materials.

Rip Blade. The rip blade is a flat-ground blade designed for cutting with the wood grain of all varieties of wood. The teeth are set alternately and are filed straight across to form a chisel-like cutting edge. Because the chisel-like teeth gouge lengths of wood fibers during ripping operations, they must be larger (fewer in number). The gullets are deeper than a typical crosscut blade. The rip blade cut is not particularly smooth, but is most useful when a great deal of ripping must be done.

Combination Blade. Radial saws usually come equipped with a *standard combination blade* which will crosscut, miter, and rip comparatively equally well. The teeth of this all purpose blade, sometimes called a *chisel-tooth flat-ground combination blade*, resemble those of a rip blade (the teeth are somewhat finer) and are set for fast cutting. Although the cut is not too smooth, it is a good blade for all-around cutting, especially for construction work.

Another popular combination blade is the so-called *novelty-tooth flat-ground combination blade*, which is divided into segments and provides either two or four cutter teeth and raker teeth in each segment, with a deep gullet between. The two-cutter type will rip a little easier than the four-cutter, but the cut is not so smooth, and it has a tendency to splinter more than the four-cutter type. However, both novelty-tooth types give a smoother cut than the standard combination blade.

In addition to these common blades, there are several specialty types. The most important of these are described here.

All-purpose Blade. The all-purpose blade (Fig. 1-16A) allows the fast, accurate cutting of hardwoods and plastic. The spe-

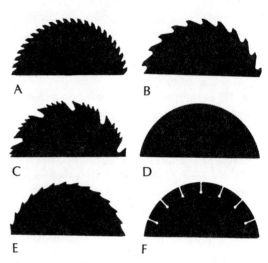

Fig. 1-16: Other popular blades include: (A) All-purpose; (B) carbide-tipped combination; (C) hollow-ground planer; (D) plywood; (E) nonferrous-metal; and (F) metal-slitting blades.

cial, hardened steel teeth make difficult ripping or crosscutting operations easier. These flame-hardened, quenched teeth stay sharp longer, but are harder to re-sharpen and do not cut as smoothly as the other combination blades.

Carbide-tipped Combination Blade. The carbide-tipped combination blade (Fig. 1-16B) rips and crosscuts like any other combination blade; however, it remains sharp for long periods of continuous operation and outlasts ordinary blades many times over. It is ideal for cutting nonferrous metals, asbestos board, hardboard, plastic, tile, plywood—as well as ordinary wood stock.

Planer Saw Blade. The planer saw blade generally has four cutting teeth and one raker, the teeth having no set. The blade is tapered or hollow-ground (Fig. 1-16C), so that it is several gauges thinner near the hub than at the rim. It is generally used by cabinetmakers when cutting stock to finish dimensions, because it cuts very smoothly both with and across the grain. The *miter blade* is similar to the planer, and is used for the same type of work.

Plywood Blade. The plywood blade (Fig. 1-16D) is a fine tooth cutting blade with either a thin-rim taper or a hollow-ground. It does an excellent job on plywood. It makes cuts with smooth finishes—ideal for glue joints and making finish cuts.

Nonferrous-metal Blade. The nonferrous-metal blade (Fig. 1-16E) is taper-ground for the smooth, free sawing of most metals except iron and steel; it is especially useful for cutting hardwoods and plastic, as well as soft nonferrous metals, including aluminum extrusions. Because chips are produced, your eyes must be protected. For best results with this

Fig. 1-17: Cut-off blade, also known as an abrasive wheel (the blade guard must always be used with the wheel).

blade, lubricate the teeth with tallow (candle wax) and feed the work slowly. The metal-slitting blade (Fig. 1-16F) is useful for the neat and accurate cutting of light sheet metal, but should not be used on thicker metals or other materials.

Cut-off Blade. The cut-off blade (Fig. 1-17) or abrasive wheel, will cut almost anything except wood. It will cut plastics, ferrous metals, nonferrous metals, stones, masonry, and ceramics. The wheel commonly used is *reinforced*, resin-bonded, and is 8 inches in diameter and about 3/32 inch thick. (Non-reinforced wheels tend to be brittle and should never be used.)

USEFUL RADIAL SAW ACCESSORIES

There are many useful commercial accessories available that will make your radial saw even more versatile. Use only recommended accessories. Consult your owner's manual for the recommended accessories for your model saw. The use of improper accessories may cause hazards.

Dado Heads. While there are several dado heads on the market, the two most popular are still the conventional dado set and the adjustable wobble blade. The conventional or standard dado set (Fig. 1-18) consists of two outside blades, each about 1/8-inch thick, whose teeth are not given any set, and inside blades, or "chippers" as they are called—one 1/4-inch thick, two 1/8-inch thick (some heads include two additional 1/8-inch chippers instead of the

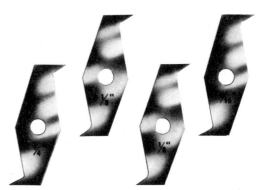

Fig. 1-18: The outside blades (Left) and inside chippers (Right) of a standard dado head.

Fig. 1-19: Adjustable dado heads, with: (A) eight carbide-tipped teeth, and (B) 24 combination teeth.

Fig. 1-20: Molding cutterhead, hex key, and sets of cutting knives.

1/4-inch one), and one 1/16-inch thick (thickness at the hub). The cutting portions of the inside cutters or chippers are widened to overlap the adjacent cutter or blade. When assembling a dado head, arrange the two outside blades so that the larger raker teeth on one are opposite the small cutting teeth on the other. This produces a smoother cutting and easier running head. Be also sure the swaged teeth of the inside cutters are placed in the gullets of the outside blades, not against the teeth, so the head cuts cleanly and the chips have exit clearance. Stagger the inside chippers so their teeth do not come together. For example, if three chippers are used, they should be set approximately 120 degrees apart. The design of the cutting teeth of the dado head set permits cutting with the grain, across the grain, or at an angle.

The second type is a single blade with self-contained adjustable wobbler units (Fig. 1-19) that can be set to cause the blade rim to wobble from side-to-side a predetermined amount as the blade revolves. These blades cut kerfs from a 3/16 inch (or 1/4 inch) minimum up to 13/16 inch and can be adjusted by rotation of a dial without removing the dado head from the saw arbor. While the dial is calibrated in 1/16-inch increments, the adjustment is continuous rather than stepped so that variations of less than 1/16 inch can be made. With most wobbler units, the arbor nut locks both the adjustment and the blade on the

arbor. These adjustable dado heads are usually available with eight carbide-tipped teeth (Fig. 1-19A) or with 24 combination teeth for high speed cutting (Fig. 1-19B).

Molding Cutterhead. The radial saw is an excellent power tool for shaping, jointing, or molding. It even offers many advantages not found with an ordinary homeshop shaper, because it can be used for shaping from the top, as well as from the side. The saw blade is replaced with a molding cutterhead (Fig. 1-20), which includes sets of formed knives or cutter shapes. A wide assortment of cutter shapes are available to fit molding heads. These shapes offer almost unlimited possibilities for shaping workpieces.

The molding cutterhead should be used with a special shaper fence (see Chapter 6), which allows the molding head to project through, and a molding head guard (Fig. 1-21), which makes it unlikely that the operator will come into contact with the cutting tool.

Accessories for Routing or Boring. The radial saw can be quickly converted into a router or boring machine. A special router bit chuck or adaptor is mounted on the auxiliary motor shaft. There are several sizes of straight right-hand router bits available for routing operations. An adaptor or chuck will also accommodate 1/2-inch diameter boring bits. However, because of the motor speed, there is some limitation on the type of bit which can be used. Mulit-spur bits, expansive bits, and auger bits more than 3/4-inch in diameter require a slower speed than that developed by the radial saw. Remember that the cutting tool and blade guard on the primary motor shaft must be removed before routing or boring can be accomplished.

Sanding accessories. Both disk and drum sanders can be attached to the primary motor shaft of the radial saw for sanding operations. The blade guard must be removed during sanding operations. On some radial saws the sanding disk is mounted on the primary shaft, but the sanding drum screws onto the auxiliary shaft end. *Always be sure there is proper ventilation in the work area when performing sanding operations.*

Buffer and Polisher. The radial saw can also be used for buffing and polishing. A buffing wheel and a pad and lamb's-wool bonnet, for polishing, are both mounted on the auxiliary motor shaft, using a geared chuck or arbor adaptor. On some radial saws, the blade and blade guard must be removed from the primary motor shaft,

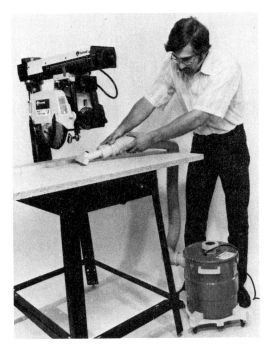

Fig. 1-22: Shop vacuum.

Fig. 1-21: Molding cutterhead guard.

and replaced with the buffing wheel, using adaptors if necessary.

Auxiliary Table Board Facing. To prevent repeated cutting into the wooden table surface, which will eventually cause the table to sag, an auxiliary table board facing can be cut and fitted onto the table. It can be made from 1/4-inch plywood or particle board and should be cut to a size that will exactly cover all of the table boards in front of the table fence. The auxiliary table board facing should be placed flat on the table and butted against the table fence. Fasten it to the table with rubber cement or an equivalent (using brads or nails is less desirable because the blade could strike them during a miter or bevel cut).

The life of the table boards will be greatly extended by the use of an auxiliary facing. The auxiliary facing can be readily replaced as often as is necessary to protect the table boards and to insure accurate and safe work.

Shop Vacuum. While not an attachment to your saw, a shop vacuum (Fig. 1-22) is an

Fig. 1-23: A typical sawdust chute.

accessory that helps keep your machine free of sawdust and other debris. This versatile device can also be used for other clean-up jobs around the shop and home.

Sawdust Chute. Although ready-built sawdust chutes are available, the one shown in Fig. 1-23 is ideal for most saws. The dimensions shown in Fig. 1-24 can be changed for adaption to your particular saw, and the design will still be quite effective. As with all jigs described in this book, the completed unit should be sanded and finished with a protective coating of polyurethane.

Safety Goggles. Safety goggles or safety glasses should be worn when operating any power tool and this includes the radial saw.

Although these are the most useful manufactured radial saw accessories and work helpers, there are other devices, less extensive in scope but extremely handy for particular jobs. Most can be easily made right in the shop. Many such devices are described in this book.

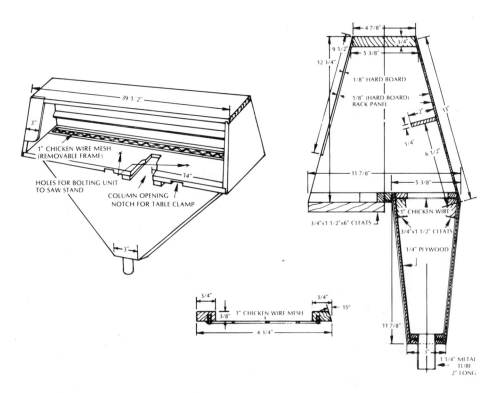

Fig. 1-24: Dimensions for a typical sawdust chute.

Chapter 2

BEFORE OPERATING THE RADIAL SAW

It is important to know your radial saw before operating it. The information in this chapter is of a general nature, applicable to most radial saws. For specific data on your radial saw, carefully check the owner's manual that came with it. By using the owner's manual along with this book, you will be able to get the most out of your radial saw.

INSTALLATION

The radial saw should be used in a location that leaves enough room to handle the size of anticipated work materials. However, the radial saw is fundamentally a one-wall shop tool, and the over-all floor space required is approximately 3 feet square (about 75 percent less operating floor space than is needed for any other machine). This design feature means that a workshop can be set up even in the smallest basement, utility room, garage, or attic. Unlike a table saw, the radial type does not require accessibility from all sides.

When locating the radial saw, space should be allowed for handling workpieces of the maximum length required. About 10 feet on either side of the center point of the column will be sufficient for most ripping operations and for the general handling of long workpieces. Only about 2 feet of operating area is required at the front of the machine. However, allow clearance for the operation of the elevating crank. Be sure to provide an ample light source, natural or artificial, to enable the easy reading of angle and dimension dials and controls. The light source should preferably be from overhead, so your shadow will not interfere with visibility.

Also, arrange to have the light fall directly on the workpiece, not in your eyes.

Radial saws generally can be purchased with or without accessory legs. If bought without the legs the radial saw can be built permanently into a workbench or placed on a steel or wood cabinet. The radial saw can also be mounted on saw horses as a temporary installation or for outdoor use. An advantage of buying the accessory legs with the radial saw is that the legs usually come equipped with leveling screws. The leveling screws can be adjusted to level the saw as shown in Fig. 2-1. This makes it possible to set up the radial saw securely on even a rough surface. Caster sets can provide additional mobility.

The correct height will vary from one shop to another because a tall person is more comfortable with a higher mounting of the saw than a short person. A height of 34 to 36 inches is a good reference point. The radial saw should be unpacked and assembled according to the manufacturer's instructions.

Fig. 2-1: A typical leveling screw on the bottom of a radial saw accessory leg.

*NOTE: To clearly illustrate certain procedures described in this chapter, the blade guard and other safety devices have been removed. To safely operate the radial saw, the guards and other safety devices must always be utilized.

To obtain the maximum efficiency from your radial saw's motor, the wire from the source of power to the machine should be of the proper size. Check with an electrician to be sure. Also, be sure that the electric line is protected with fuses or circuit breakers. If an ordinary type of fuse blows during the initial fraction of a second when the machine is turned on, do not put in a new one of higher rating. Instead, replace it with a fuse of the same rating, but of the "slow-blow" or delay type which contains a special fusible link that withstands a momentary overload without giving way.

Before plugging the cord into the wall or floor outlet, look at the nameplate on your machine to see that its voltage supply needs are the same as that in the workshop. If you ordered a radial saw for use on a 120-volt line, be sure the nameplate is marked 120 volts. Unless the voltage is delivered to within plus or minus ten percent of the motor nameplate rating, operation may not be satisfactory. If the motor runs hot or is short of power, call your local power company to check your voltage.

The radial saw, as with any other power tool, should always be electrically grounded while in use. This precaution will protect the operator against possible electric shock should a short circuit or ground develop while the tool is being connected to the power outlet or during operation of the tool. Most radial saws offer assured grounding protection for your safety. In accordance with a requirement of the National Electric Code, it is equipped with a three-wire cord, one wire being a ground wire. For your complete safety while operating this saw, remember that the three-conductor attachment plug naturally requires a three-prong outlet (Fig. 2-2A). Just insert the three-prong plug, and the machine is instantly grounded if the receptacle is properly installed.

To permit use of this machine with a two-prong receptacle, an adaptor (Fig. 2-2B) is available (such adaptors are not applicable in Canada). When using the adaptor, the

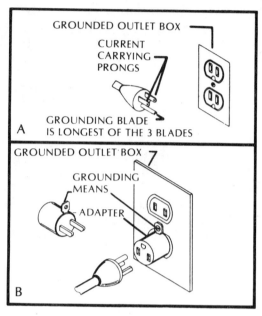

Fig. 2-2: (A) Grounded outlet, and (B) grounding adaptor.

extending green wire should be connected to the outlet-plate retaining screw, provided that the outlet itself is grounded, or to any other known permanent ground, such as a water or electric-conduct pipe. **Caution: If an extension cord is used, be sure it is a three-wire cord and large enough to prevent excessive voltage loss.**

If there are young children in the family, it is wise to make your radial saw "kid-proof." Most manufacturers provide an aid to accomplish this vital safety "must." For instance, some saws are equipped with a special switch, as shown in Fig. 2-3, that locks the saw when it is in the "OFF" position. This can be done by grasping the switch toggle and pulling it out of the switch. With the switch toggle removed, the switch will not operate. However, should the switch toggle be removed while the saw is running, the saw can be turned "OFF" once, but cannot be restarted without inserting the switch toggle. Some manufacturers provide a special safety key which must be inserted and used to unlock the ON/OFF switch, before the saw can be turned on. With other radial saws the key must be inserted and turned to the ON position, before the saw can be switched on in the normal manner. Regardless of the type of ON/OFF switch protection your saw has, be sure to use it to keep your saw "kidproof."

SAW ADJUSTMENTS

Usually the instruction manual which comes with the machine describes how to make adjustments. The following adjustment procedures are general in nature; since specific adjustments vary from machine to machine, check your owner's manual for *exact* instructions. Remember, however, when making adjustments on a radial saw, **always disconnect the machine from the power source.**

Regardless of the care with which you use your machine, normal strain and the abrasive action of dust and dirt will cause moving parts to wear, which will eventually throw the machine out of alignment. Sooner or later, adjustment and realignment are necessary to maintain accuracy in any machine.

Checking the Table Fence for Accuracy. For accurate work, the table fence must be straight. The tableboards should be checked with a straightedge and made straight by jointing or sanding before other adjustments are made. When checking the table fence for accuracy, be sure that the tableboard clamps at the rear of the table are tightened. Also, the front tableboard must be flat. This can be checked with a straightedge and leveled by using the table adjusting screws to raise or lower the center of the table if it is bowed down or up (Fig. 2-4).

The most frequently used position for the table fence on the worktable is shown

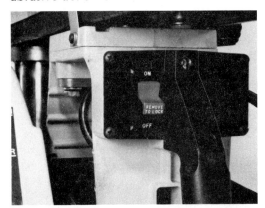

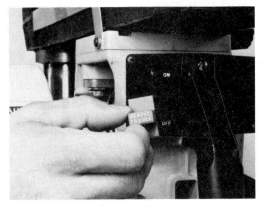

Fig. 2-3: A special switch that can be locked in the OFF position.

Fig. 2-4: Table adjusting screws to raise or lower the center of the worktable.

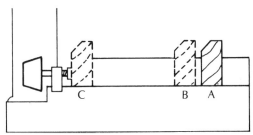

Fig. 2-5: The worktable: (A) in the standard position; (B) with the table fence behind the spacer board; and (C) with the table fence at the rear of the worktable.

by position A in Fig. 2-5. This will usually be sufficient for average cutting jobs. If you want the maximum crosscut on 1-inch material or wider bevel-miter capacity, loosen the tableboard clamps at the rear of the table top and relocate the table fence behind the spacer board as shown by position B. Tighten the clamps after this change has been made.

For maximum width when ripping, loosen the clamps and relocate the table fence by placing it at the rear of the table top and near the column base, as shown by position C. Again, tighten the clamps to hold the table fence firmly in place.

Leveling the Saw. The radial saw should be level from side to side and tilted very slightly towards the rear of the machine—back, toward the column—to prevent the cuttinghead from free-rolling toward the operator. If the saw is mounted on accessory legs, adjust the leveling screws until the saw stands firmly in the correct position. Then tighten the lock nuts on the leveling screws. If the saw is mounted on a bench, place shims between the saw base and the bench to achieve the correct position and then securely bolt the saw to the bench. Loosen the carriage clamp knob and test the cuttinghead to be sure it will not free-roll forward. Slightly more effort should be required to pull the cuttinghead

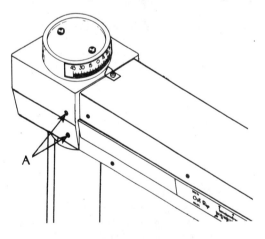

Fig. 2-6: Screws for adjusting the radial arm lock tension.

forward than to push it to the return position.

Also, if during any cutting operation, with the cuttinghead in any possible position, there is any tendency for the tool to tip over or to slide or walk on the supporting surface, the stand or bench must be secured to the floor.

Adjusting the Radial Arm Lock Tension. The tension on the radial arm locking mechanism is set at the factory; however, it can be adjusted. If the radial arm does not fall easily into the lock positions as it is swiveled on the column, very slightly loosen the two adjusting screws shown in Fig. 2-6 with an Allen wrench. If "play" exists in the lock positions or if the arm feels loose, very slightly tighten the two adjusting screws.

Adjusting the Blade Square with the Table Top. Remove the blade guard and place the cuttinghead in the normal crosscut position. Lower the blade to just clear the table and slide the cuttinghead forward until the blade is over the fixed front tableboard. Clamp the cuttinghead in this position with the carriage clamp knob. Be sure the motor and blade are locked in the horizontal position—with the bevel angle scale at 0 degrees—and the bevel clamp handle is tightened. Place a steel square on the table and against the saw blade as shown in Fig. 2-7. Be sure the square is flush against the side of the blade and not riding on the edge of a blade tooth. If the blade is not square with the table, remove the bevel scale plate at the front of the cuttinghead by loosening two round head screws. Slightly loosen the hex head screws behind the bevel scale plate. Tilt the motor until the blade is flush with the square (remember, the square must be between the teeth of the blade) and tighten the hex head screws. Replace the bevel scale plate and adjust the pointer to the 0 degree mark on the scale.

On some radial saws, the bolts between the motor and the motor bracket must be loosened. Then the cuttinghead must be

Fig. 2-7: *Using a steel square for adjusting the blade square with the table top.*

grasped in both hands and the motor tilted in the direction necessary to square the blade. After the bolts have been retightened, the pointer on the bevel angle scale should be set to the 0 degree mark on the scale as in the first procedure. Always replace the blade guard after squaring the blade with the table.

Adjusting the Saw Blade Travel Square with the Fence. Remove the blade guard and the saw blade. Then place one of the wrenches supplied with the saw between the blade collars (arbor flanges) as shown in Fig. 2-8. Lock the radial arm in the nor-

mal crosscut position, and place the pointer on the miter scale at the 0 degree mark. Lower the radial arm until the wrench just clears the table surface and place a framing square on the table with one end of the square against the fence and the other end against the wrench. Loosen the carriage clamp knob and slide the cuttinghead the length of the radial arm, and watch to see if the wrench travels parallel to the square. If it does not, an adjustment is necessary. First, loosen the two screws at the top of the column base (Fig. 2-9A). If the arm must be moved to the right (when facing the rear of the saw), loosen the two screws on the left side of the column base (Fig. 2-9B) and tighten the two screws on the right side (Fig. 2-9C). To adjust the arm to the left (again, facing the rear of the saw), loosen the two right-hand screws (Fig. 2-9C) and tighten the two left-hand ones (Fig 2-9B). When you are certain that the saw blade is square with the fence, make sure that the elevating crank operates smoothly. If it sticks or jerks, further adjustment can be made by adjusting the same screws (Fig. 2-9B and C), being careful to keep the saw blade square with the table fence. Tighten the two screws (Fig. 2-9A) and move the miter scale until the 0 degree mark lines up with the pointer.

Fig. 2-8: *Using an arbor nut wrench and steel square to check the accuracy of the saw blade travel.*

Fig. 2-9: *Adjusting the saw blade travel square with the fence.*

Removing "Heeling" in the Saw Cut.
Even though the cuttinghead may be correctly aligned at 90 degrees to the table fence, the blade itself may not be square with the table fence. This occurs when the yoke is not square in the carriage to the table fence. This condition causes what is known as "heeling" (Fig. 2-10) in the saw cut. To check and adjust for heeling, proceed in the following manner.

Remove the blade guard. Replace the table fence with a piece of 3/4 inch plywood at least 5 inches high (Fig. 2-11). Tighten the table board clamps. Then, place three short pieces of 2 x 4 inch stock

Fig. 2-11: Checking to see if the blade is square with the table fence.

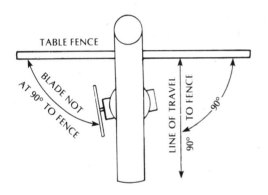

Fig. 2-10: "Heeling" in the saw cut.

on the table and lay a framing square on them so that the short arm of the square is flush against the plywood fence and the long arm of the square is flush against the blade. Be certain the square is between the teeth of the blade.

If the blade is not parallel to the square, an adjustment is necessary. Release the yoke clamp handle and loosen the two hex head screws on the underside of the yoke (Fig. 2-12). Swivel the yoke until the blade is parallel with the square and tighten the yoke clamp handle; then retighten the two hex head screws.

Adjustment of the Ball Bearings Against the Track in the Radial Arm. The cuttinghead is suspended, by the carriage, from three lubricated, shielded ball bearings, two on fixed shafts, and the third bearing—

on the saw blade side of the cuttinghead—on an adjustable eccentric shaft.

After years of operation, wear may develop in the track arm, causing "play" between the ball bearings and the tracks on which they ride. Check the ball bearings against the track for any looseness or unevenness. The ball bearings must ride smoothly and evenly in the track for the saw to cut accurately. To check for "play," and to adjust the bearings on the eccentric shaft to eliminate it, use the following steps.

Loosen the radial arm end cap (at the front of the arm), and remove the screws

Fig. 2-12: Two hex head screws are used to adjust for "heeling."

Fig. 2-13: To eliminate looseness or "play" between the ball bearings and the track, the eccentric shaft must be turned.

Fig. 2-15: Adjusting the in-rip scale.

holding the sheet metal cover from the top of the arm. Take the cover off of the arm. Loosen the now exposed retaining nut on the adjustable bearing (Fig. 2-13A). Turn the eccentric shaft (Fig. 2-13B) clockwise to eliminate the looseness or "play." Retighten the retaining nut. Check for any "play," but make certain the carriage moves freely on the track. Replace the sheet metal cover on the arm, and tighten the screws fixing the end cap to the arm.

Adjusting the Out-Rip Scale. Place and clamp the table fence in the rearmost position. Rotate the yoke to put the blade in the out-rip position and tighten the yoke clamp handle. Lower the blade until it just clears the table and slide the carriage along the arm to the front of the saw (Fig. 2-14). Measure 24 inches from the table fence

Fig. 2-14: Adjusting the out-rip scale.

and adjust the cuttinghead so that the inside edge of the blade teeth is 24 inches from the fence. The retractable leaf guard must be pushed out of the way when measuring from the fence to the blade. Next tighten the carriage clamp knob, and set the out-rip pointer at the 24 inch mark on the out-rip scale.

Adjusting the In-Rip Scale. Place and clamp the table fence in the rearmost position. Rotate the yoke to the in-rip position, and tighten the yoke clamp handle. Lower the cuttinghead until the blade just clears the table, then slide the carriage to the back end of the arm (towards the column) until the blade is flush against the table fence (Fig. 2-15). The retractable leaf guard must be lifted to clear the table fence. Tighten the carriage clamp knob, and set the in-rip pointer at the 0 inch mark of the in-rip scale.

Mounting the Saw Blade and Blade Guard. Saw blades and most other circular cutting tools are mounted directly on the radial saw motor shaft, which is itself the arbor. To mount a cutting tool, remove the arbor nut and arbor collars using the wrenches supplied with the saw (Fig. 2-16). One wrench holds the arbor from turning, the other turns the nut, *clockwise*, until it is loose. Elevate the radial arm until the blade will slide on the shaft and clear the table top. Then place the 3/8-inch arbor collar on the arbor, with the recessed side

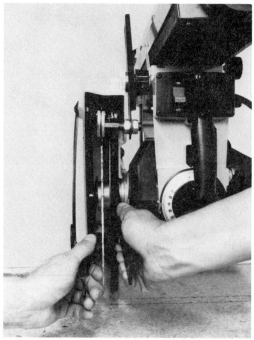

Fig. 2-16: Using special arbor nut wrenches to remove the saw blade.

of the collar against the saw blade. Place the saw blade on the arbor with the teeth pointing in the direction of the motor's rotation. For example, if the arm is perpendicular to the table fence and the blade is parallel to the arm in the normal cross-cutting position, the teeth should rotate out towards the operator and down into a workpiece.

After putting the blade on the arbor, place the 1/4-inch outside arbor collar on the arbor with the recessed side against the saw blade. Replace the arbor nut. Place a wrench on the flat of the arbor shaft to hold it, and tighten the arbor nut with the arbor-nut wrench. The arbor nut found on most saws has a left-hand Acme thread, which means that the nut must be turned and tightened *counter-clockwise.*

When the blade is secure, mount the blade guard on the motor housing, and adjust it to the proper position for the cuts you are going to make. Be sure to properly tighten the blade guard clamp knob.

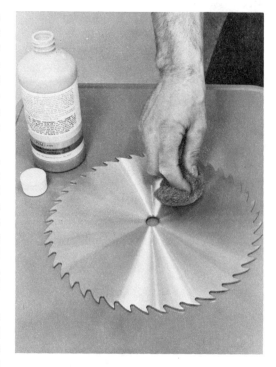

Fig. 2-17: Cleaning a saw blade with solvent.

Other Maintenance Tips. Although the radial saw requires only minimal maintenance, the following checks should be made on occasion to make sure problems do not arise:

1. Check all nuts, bolts, and screws for tightness. Check all moving parts: turning, rotating, sliding, or cranking, to make certain these are functioning properly.

2. Check the motor shaft (which is also the saw arbor), to be sure it is not bent or loose.

3. Make sure all safety devices operate properly and easily. Many safety devices, for instance, the anti-kickback fingers and splitter, not only help to protect the operator; they also facilitate efficient cutting operations.

4. Regular oil or grease is *not* recommended for the lubrication of any of the moving parts of the saw, because it would only serve to catch sawdust and clog the rotating and sliding mechanisms. Instead, use one of the available silicone products or powdered graphite for the lubrication of moving parts.

5. Keep all working parts and the motor free from sawdust and other substances that might have an abrasive effect on the parts. Also, always keep the worktable surface clean, and do not allow sawdust to accumulate around the base of the saw or workbench.

6. Blade teeth tend to become clogged with sawdust and resin. This causes dragging during the cut. Clean your blades frequently, using a resin solvent when necessary (Fig. 2-17), and apply a light coating of rust preventative.

TROUBLESHOOTING GUIDE

In spite of how well a radial saw is maintained, problems do occasionally occur. The following troubleshooting guide will help solve the more common problems.

Trouble: *Saw will not start.*

Probable Cause	Remedy
1. Saw not plugged in.	1. Plug in saw.
2. Fuse blown or circuit breaker tripped.	2. Replace fuse or reset circuit breaker.
3. Cord damaged.	3. Have cord replaced.
4. Overload relay or protector not set.	4. Push overload reset button.
5. Bad capacitor or starting relay.	5. Have capacitor or starting relay replaced.
6. Low voltage.	6. Check power line for proper voltage.

Trouble: *Overload kicks out frequently.*

Probable Cause	Remedy
1. Extension cord too light or too long.	1. Replace with adequate size cord.
2. Cutting stock too fast.	2. Cut stock more slowly.
3. Blade in poor condition (dull, warped, gummed).	3. Clean or replace blade.
4. Blade binding because of misaligned table fence.	4. Check and adjust table fence.
5. Blade binding because of warped wood.	5. Select another piece of wood.
6. Low supply voltage.	6. Contact your electric company.

TROUBLESHOOTING GUIDE (Cont.)

Trouble: *Motor overheats.*

Probable Cause	Remedy
1. Steps 1 through 6 under "overload kicks out frequently."	1. Same as 1 through 6 under "overload kicks out frequently."
2. Sawdust blocking air flow through motor.	2. Brush or blow out sawdust.
3. Too many lights, electric equipment on circuit.	3. Use separate circuit for saw or reduce line load.

Trouble: *Fuse blows or circuit breaker trips repeatedly.*

Probable Cause	Remedy
1. Too many lights, electric equipment on circuit.	1. Use separate circuit for saw or reduce line load.
2. Inadequate fuse for circuit.	2. Replace with time lag fuse.
3. Short circuit in motor junction box, line cord or plug, or loose connections.	3. Check for worn or damaged cord insulation or loose connections causing shorted wires. Have all terminals in motor junction box inspected for loose or shortened connections.

Trouble: *Saw does not come up to speed or develop full power.*

Probable Cause	Remedy
1. Extension cord too light or too long.	1. Replace with adequate size cord.
2. Low supply voltage.	2. Contact your electric company.
3. Motor wired for different voltage.	3. Make sure motor and supply are the same voltage.
4. Too many lights, electric equipment on circuit.	4. Use separate circuit for saw or reduce line load.
5. Starting relay not operating.	5. Have relay replaced.
6. Bad capacitor.	6. Have capacitor replaced.
7. Incorrect fuses in power line.	7. Install correct fuses.

Trouble: *Starting relay in motor will not operate.*

Probable Cause	Remedy
1. Burned relay contacts (because of extended hold-in periods caused by low line voltage).	1. Have relay replaced and have line voltage checked.
2. Open relay coil.	2. Have replay replaced.
3. Loose or broken connections in motor terminal box.	3. Have wiring checked and repaired.

Trouble: *Motor stalls (resulting in blown fuses or tripped circuit breakers).*

Probable Cause	Remedy
1. Starting relay not operating.	1. Have relay replaced.
2. Voltage too low to permit motor to reach operating speed.	2. Have the low line voltage condition corrected.
3. Fuses or circuit breakers do not have sufficient capacity.	3. Replace fuses or circuit breakers with proper capacity units.
4. Cutting too fast.	4. Cut slower.

TROUBLESHOOTING GUIDE (Cont.)

Trouble: *Frequent opening of fuses or circuit breakers.*

Probable Cause	Remedy
1. Motor overloaded.	1. Reduce motor load.
2. Fuses or circuit breakers do not have sufficient capacity.	2. Replace fuses or circuit breakers.
3. Starting relay not operating (motor does not reach normal speed).	3. Have relay replaced.

Trouble: *Saw makes unsatisfactory cuts.*

Probable Cause	Remedy
1. Dull blade.	1. Replace blade.
2. Blade mounted backwards.	2. Turn blade around.
3. Gum or pitch on blade.	3. Remove blade and clean with turpentine and coarse steel wool.
4. Incorrect blade for work being done.	4. Change the blade.
5. Gum or pitch on worktable causing erratic feed.	5. Clean worktable.
6. Blade not properly sharpened.	6. Replace or sharpen blade.

Trouble: *Saw does not make accurate 45 and 90 degree crosscuts or bevel cuts.*

Probable Cause	Remedy
1. Cuttinghead bearings out of adjustment.	1. Check and adjust cuttinghead bearings.
2. Worktable mounting brackets not adjusted correctly.	2. Check and adjust worktable mounting brackets.
3. Table not flat.	3. Check and adjust table for flatness.
4. Saw blade travel not square with table fence.	4. Check and adjust saw blade.
5. Blade not square with worktable.	5. Check blade with square and adjust.
6. Blade causing "heeling" in cuts.	6. Check and adjust blade, square with table fence.

Trouble: *Saw does not make accurate rip cuts.*

Probable Cause	Remedy
1. Steps 1 through 6 under "45 and 90 degree crosscuts or bevel cuts."	1. Same as 1 through 6 under "45 and 90 degree crosscuts and bevel cuts."
2. Rip scale pointers not adjusted properly.	2. Check and adjust "in-rip" and "out-rip" scale pointers.
3. Material not guided against table fence.	3. Always use table fence to guide material when ripping.
4. Carriage clamp knob not tight.	4. Tighten carriage clamp knob securely.

Trouble: *Material pinches blade when ripping.*

Probable Cause	Remedy
1. Splitter not in place.	1. Install and use splitter.
2. Warped wood.	2. Select another piece of wood.
3. Insufficient set on blade.	3. Reset or replace blade.

TROUBLESHOOTING GUIDE (Cont.)

Trouble: *Material binds on splitter.*

Probable Cause	Remedy
1. Splitter not aligned correctly with blade.	1. Check and align splitter with blade.

Trouble: *Machine vibrates excessively.*

Probable Cause	Remedy
1. Saw not mounted securely to stand or workbench.	1. Tighten all mounting hardware.
2. Stand or bench on uneven floor.	2. Reposition on flat level surface; fasten to floor if necessary.
3. Damaged saw blade.	3. Replace blade.

Trouble: *Material kicks back from blade when ripping.*

Probable Cause	Remedy
1. Splitter not aligned with blade.	1. Align splitter with blade.
2. Material not guided against table fence.	2. Always use table fence to guide material when ripping.
3. Splitter not in place.	3. Install and use splitter.
4. Dull or pitch-coated blade.	4. Replace or clean blade.
5. Letting go of material before it is past saw blade.	5. Push material all the way past the saw blade before releasing work.
6. Anti-kickback fingers dull.	6. Sharpen anti-kickback fingers.
7. Warped wood.	7. Select another piece of wood.

Trouble: *Radial arm does not raise or lower freely.*

Probable Cause	Remedy
1. Too much tension on elevating column.	1. Adjust tension on elevating column.
2. No lubrication on elevating column.	2. Apply a light coating of silicone or graphite to elevating column.

Trouble: *Carriage does not roll smoothly on radial arm.*

Probable Cause	Remedy
1. Dirt on tracks.	1. Clean tracks.
2. Carriage bearings out of adjustment.	2. Check and adjust the carriage bearings.

Trouble: *Blade does not stop within a few seconds after turning off the saw.*

Probable Cause	Remedy
1. Brake lining is worn out.	1. Have brake lining replaced.

SAFETY AND THE RADIAL SAW

Safety and craftsmanlike work are both dependent on a thorough knowledge of your tool and the proper methods of using it. As mentioned earlier, the radial saw is easy to use, but like all power tools certain safety precautions must be taken. Using the radial saw with the respect and caution demanded will considerably lessen the possibility of personal injury. However, if normal safety precautions are overlooked or completely ignored, the operator could possibly be injured or the radial saw could be damaged.

As a guide for the radial saw operator, the following safety precautions are important.

1. Know your radial saw. Read the owner's manual very carefully. Learn the saw's applications and limitations, as well as the specific potential hazards associated with its use.

2. Avoid a dangerous environment. Do not use the radial saw in damp or wet locations, or expose it to rain. Keep your work area well-lighted.

3. Tighten all clamps and levers before starting the machine, and make no adjustments while the saw is running. In fact, always disconnect the tool before making adjustments and when changing accessories such as blades and cutters. This will avoid accidental starting.

4. Maintain the radial saw in top condition. Keep it clean for the best and safest performance. Never use a dull saw blade or one that does not have sufficient set. Also, be sure to keep the machine in good alignment and adjustment to prevent excessive vibration which will cause inaccurate cutting and cause the saw to grab or creep.

5. Check damaged parts. Before using a cutting tool, guard, or other part that is damaged, carefully check to ensure that it will operate properly and perform its intended function. Check for alignment of moving parts, binding of moving parts, breakage of parts, mounting, and any other conditions that may affect its operation. A guard or other part that is damaged should be properly repaired or replaced.

6. Dress properly. Jewelry, neckties, loose clothing, long sleeves, or gloves can get caught in the cutting tool or workpiece. Nonslip footwear is recommended. A hair-net is recommended for long hair.

7. Use safety glasses or goggles. Also, wear a face shield or dust mask if the cutting operation is dusty. When using the saw for extended periods of operation, wear earplugs or earmuffs.

8. Leave no tools or pieces of wood on the worktable when the radial saw is in operation, and keep the floor around the machine clean and in good condition.

9. Always use the blade guard with the proper adjustment when operating the radial saw. Also, make sure the anti-kickback fingers and splitter are in the proper position when ripping. The guard should be lowered on the infeed end and the anti-kickback attachment properly adjusted when ripping. Position the dust spout so that dust and chips are directed away from the operator.

10. Never perform any operation "freehand," which means using only your hands to support or guide the workpiece. Always use the table fence as a back stop for crosscutting and a guide edge for ripping.

11. Stock should not be removed from the table until the saw has been returned to the rear of the table. Always use a stick for removing small pieces of scrap from the worktable. You should never get your hands in the path of the blade's travel. Never reach behind or over the moving cutting tool with either hand for any reason.

12. When crosscutting, move the blade or cutter into the workpiece against the direction or rotation of the blade or cutter only. Do not force the saw. It will do the job better and be safer at the rate for which it was designed. When finished crosscutting, always return the cuttinghead to the rear of the arm.

13. When ripping, the direction of the rotation of the saw blade will be upward toward the operator. Always feed the workpiece past the safety guard from the side opposite the anti-kickback fingers. In other words, you must feed the workpiece into the blade or cutter against the direction of the rotation of the blade or cutter. Always follow the warning or diagram for blade direction on the blade guard, to be absolutely certain of not ripping from the wrong end.

14. Use a pushstick when ripping or when cutting with the molding cutterhead if there is any doubt of finger clearance. Provide adequate support to the front and sides of the saw table for wide or long workpieces.

15. When making any kind of cut, keep yourself in a balanced position. If you are crosscutting material from the left, put your left foot forward and place your left hand approximately 12 inches to the left of the line of blade travel. Pull the yoke handle with the right hand. If you are cutting from the right side, put your right foot forward and hold the material with your right hand, then pull the yoke handle with your left hand. Avoid awkward operations and hand positions where a sudden slip could cause your hand to move into the cutting tool.

16. Never force the dado head into its cut. Because more stock is being removed, only a very slight pull is required. When crosscutting heavy stock, or cross-dadoing, tools will have a tendency to climb-cut or move forward without pulling. You may have to hold the cuttinghead back.

17. Use clamps to hold workpieces when practical. It is safer than using your hand and frees both hands to operate the saw. Also, never attempt to free a stalled saw blade without first turning the switch to "OFF" and disconnecting the saw from the power source.

18. Do not take your eyes off the work you are doing, and do not talk to anyone while using the radial saw. All children and visitors should be kept a safe distance from the work area. Make sure the tool is kid-proof.

19. Never leave the radial saw running unattended. Turn the power to the "OFF" position and watch the tool come to a complete stop, before leaving the saw. Make sure the switch is in the "OFF" position before plugging in the cord.

20. Do not operate a radial saw while under the influence of drugs, alcohol, or any medication. Continual alertness is most important when operating any power tool.

Chapter 3

BASIC OPERATION OF THE RADIAL SAW

The radial saw is basically a pull-through cutoff type of saw, that cuts in a straight line. Although the different types of saw cuts that may be made with the radial saw seem endless in number, as mentioned in Chapter 1, they are really combinations of the six basic woodworking saw cuts—crosscut, bevel crosscut, miter, bevel miter (compound), rip, and bevel rip. In fact, as shown in Fig. 3-1, all six cuts are made on the radial saw by two actions—crosscutting and ripping.

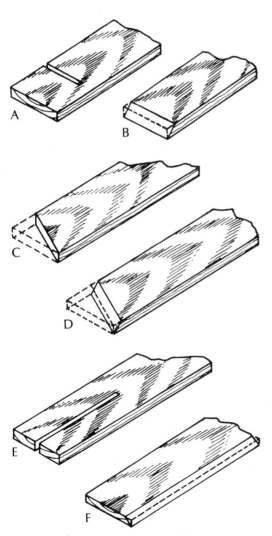

Before continuing with the operation of the radial saw, it might be wise to define both the crosscutting and ripping actions as they apply to this machine. As we know, commercial stock lumber has the grain of the wood running with the length of the board. Originally, "cross-cutting" meant making any cut across the grain or short dimension of the board. "Ripping" has traditionally meant making a cut with the grain, through the length of the board, resulting in two narrower pieces. However, these definitions do not apply to "action" accomplished on a radial saw.

During the crosscutting action, the radial saw blade is moved toward the operator. Therefore, the saw blade's thrust is down and toward the column at the back of the saw (Fig. 3-2A). This climb cut action holds the work firmly against the table fence when performing the normal crosscutting sawing action.

When ripping with the radial saw, the cutting action is always *against* the feed so that the saw does not pull the work forward at the blade speed (Fig. 3-2B). All of the parts of the cuttinghead are locked in a stationary position. The feed is against the rotation of the saw blade. The anti-kickback fingers on the saw blade guard

Fig. 3-1: The six basic woodworking saw cuts: (A) crosscut; (B) bevel crosscut; (C) miter; (D) bevel miter (compound angle); (E) rip; (F) bevel rip.

*NOTE: *To clearly illustrate certain procedures described in this chapter, the blade guard and other safety devices have been removed. To safely operate the radial saw, the guards and other safety devices must always be utilized.*

tend to prevent a "kickback" toward the operator. It should be noted again that a radial saw should be used only with all safety devices, particularly the blade guards. In many photographs in this book the lower retractable leaf guard has been removed for the sake of clarity. *Use all guards and safety devices recommended by the manufacturer.*

The radial saw can perform two kinds of cuts which cannot be done on any other kind of stationary power tool without special jigs. These are made on the radial saw with the blade in a horizontal position. If the carriage is moved the same as when

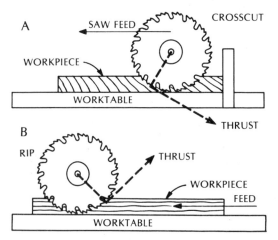

Fig. 3-2: The thrust of the saw blade: (A) when crosscutting; (B) when ripping.

crosscutting, the operation is called "end cutting." If the workpiece is fed into the blade as in ripping, the operation is known as "edge cutting." Nevertheless, these cuts (Fig. 3-3) are still only variations of the basic ones.

Auxiliary Table Boards. In Chapter 1, it was recommended that you attach an auxiliary table board facing, also known as a scarfing board, to the worktable. Because through-sawing requires the blade to cut into the top of the worktable, the table will eventually be destroyed by the cuts. Never use a badly cut up table fence for ripping, because workpieces can easily snag as they

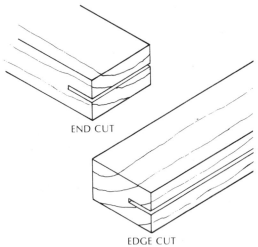

Fig. 3-3: End and edge cutting are done with the saw blade in a horizontal position.

slide along it. Also, a badly cut up front table board makes it difficult to align workpieces for crosscutting operations. Since cuts into the table should never be greater than 1/16-inch in depth, a piece of 1/4-inch thick plywood or hardboard is an ideal replaceable table board.

Because the worktable or the auxiliary table board facing will automatically receive cuts during sawing operations, it is a good idea to precut the common table grooves, as shown in Fig. 3-4. Pre-prepared

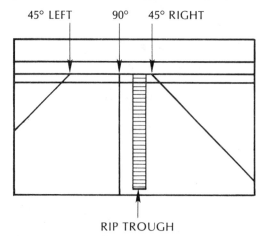

Fig. 3-4: It is a good idea to precut the common worktable grooves.

grooves make the first cutting operation easier, and they help to ensure accuracy during any cutting operation. The rip trough should extend from the fence to the front of the front table board, so that the ripping operation can be easily done in any position along the radial arm.

The table or guide fence must always be

A

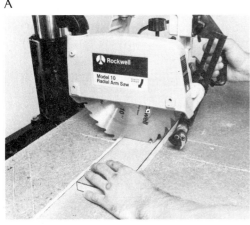

B

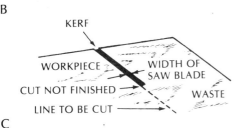

C

Fig. 3-5: Using (A) a left-hand feed; or (B) a right-hand feed when crosscutting on the radial saw; (C) for any cut the kerf should be on the waste side.

at least one-half the height of the workpiece. If the regular guide fence is not high enough for any cutting operation, a higher table fence should be substituted. A special worktable should always be used when dadoing horizontally or when using the molding cutterhead. The designs of these special auxiliary tables are described later in the book.

CROSSCUTTING ACTION

The radial saw is designed for pulling the carriage away from the column and the back of the arm, toward the front of the saw when crosscutting. There are several advantages to this type of cutting motion. The direction of the thrust of the saw blade forces the workpiece down on the table and back against the table fence, where it will be firmly and safely positioned. When pulling, the saw blade rotates in the same direction as the travel of the carriage along the arm, causing the blade to feed itself somewhat. This makes for greater ease when cutting. However, with thick or gummy workpieces, this tendency for the blade to self-feed may be so great that the operator will have to hold the blade back instead of feeding it into the workpiece. Also, when pulling, the cut begins at the table fence which supports the workpiece enough to prevent the splintering of its edge.

Either hand may be used to pull the carriage along the arm when crosscutting. You may have a tendency to use a left-hand feed because it puts the holding (right) hand on the side away from the saw (Fig. 3-5A). However, a right-hand feed (Fig. 3-5B) generally is more practical and more comfortable, and is usually quickly adopted by most right-handed operators. Remember to never cross your arms. Stand with the shoulder of the arm pulling the carriage directly in front of the end of the arm of the saw. Always keep the hand holding the workpiece away from the blade. For some cutting operations, it may be more comfortable to employ a different hand feed than the one you usually use. This is perfectly all right, as long as you know the line of the cut and are careful to keep your holding hand out of this line. Also, remember that the long part of the work should always be on the side of the holding hand. For example, the long part of the material would be on the left, since you would be holding it down with your left hand. The other (cutoff) side must be free to slide away from the saw blade as it is cut off. Don't forget that the kerf has width; therefore, be sure to locate the workpiece so that the kerf is on the waste side (Fig. 3-5C).

The anti-kickback fingers are not needed to prevent kickback when crosscutting. In fact, they should not be touching the workpiece; however it is best to allow them to hang down on the arm holding them to within an 1/8 inch of the workpiece, to act as a frontal blade guard.

Straight Crosscutting. When straight crosscutting, the radial arm must be at right angles with the table fence—indicated as 0 degrees on the miter scale. Locate the radial arm index knob in the column slot at the 0-degree position, and then securely lock the arm with the radial arm clamp knob. Now the saw blade should follow the saw kerf in the table top. Use the elevating crank to drop the saw blade until the teeth are approximately 1/32 to 1/16 inch below the top surface of the table in the saw kerf. This clearance is needed to cut through the board. Then return the saw all the way back against the column. For normal crosscutting, the fence is placed in the standard position. It may be positioned as far back as the column when greater capacity is required for wide material or "gang cutting."

Place the workpiece on the table against the guide fence. Position the guard so that it is parallel to the work surface with the kickback fingers about 1/8 inch above the material being cut. Turn on the power and give the motor sufficient time to attain full speed. Always hold the workpiece firmly on the table and against the table or guide

Fig. 3-6: Method of straight crosscutting on the radial saw.

fence with the holding hand. Then pull the saw blade from behind the table fence, in one steady motion, completely through the line of the cut (Fig. 3-6). Do not bring it through too fast; rather, allow it to cut smoothly and completely at its own feeding speed to avoid overheating and "blade walking." Once the stock is severed, do not pull the saw forward any further. Instead, push the saw to the rear of the fence before removing the workpiece from the table. Practice, to get the "feel" of the cutting action—let the saw blade do the cutting—never force it!

Crosscutting is generally done to produce a piece to exact length or to square an end. When setting up the machine to perform these operations, it is advisable to cut through the fence, then mark the fence and table so that the fence can be easily returned to the same position should it be removed. In most cases, since cutting is done to a mark, work can then be readily positioned to line up with the kerf in the fence and table before starting the saw.

To crosscut a piece of slightly bowed stock, place the concave (hollow) side down on the table, to prevent the workpiece from rocking. Hold one edge of the stock down on the table. Do not attempt to crosscut a bowed workpiece if it cannot be held firmly on the worktable when cutting.

Crosscutting Oversized Stock. One of the great advantages of the radial saw is the ability to crosscut any length board you have the space to handle. But, if the workpiece overhangs the table at one or both ends to any extent, it is necessary to support the overhanging end or ends, to prevent them from seesawing upward while the workpiece is being cut. A sawhorse or any support which is the same height as the worktable is an inexpensive accessory for this type of operation (Fig. 3-7).

A

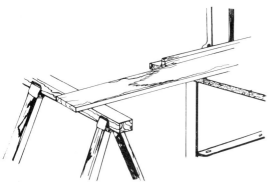

Fig. 3-7: Supporting the end of a long workpiece when crosscutting.

To crosscut stock beyond the capacity of the machine with the fence in the standard fence position, make the first pass to the full travel of the blade. After the blade has been returned behind the fence and has come to a complete stop, flop the board over (other side up) so that the opposite edge is against the table fence, for the second pass. For the accurate crosscutting of wide boards, use a stop block arrangement to locate the length desired (Fig. 3-8A). Then cut as far as possible on one side of the workpiece, turning it over and positioning it against the stop block to complete the cut (Fig. 3-8B). Frequently, it may be necessary to relocate the fence to its "back" position and to situate the workpiece with the blade in the kerf already made. In such cases, the second pass made is really an extension of the first cut (Fig. 3-8C). More information about cutting wide panels can be found later in this

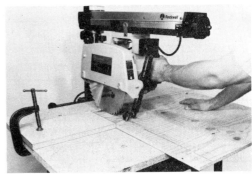

B

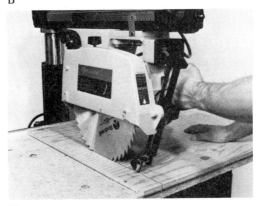

C

Fig. 3-8: (A) Using a stop block to locate the length desired when crosscutting a wide board (the workpiece must be square); (B) turning the stock over and positioning it against the stop block for the second cut; (C) cutting a wide board with the table fence in the rear position, making the second pass an extension of the first cut.

chapter and in Chapter 5.

To crosscut a workpiece thicker than the capacity of the machine, set the blade just a little more than half the thickness of the material (Fig. 3-9A). Pull the blade through the workpiece the same way as for straight crosscutting, and then turn it over, and complete the cut on the other side. When turning the material over, line its kerf with that on the table top and in the table fence to assure a square cut (Fig. 3-9B). For accuracy, use a stop block, keeping the same workpiece end against the stop block for both passes of the saw. Flop the workpiece over, so that the opposite edge is against the table fence for the second cut. The end of the stock must be square to ensure proper location.

When the thickness of the material is greater than the capacity of the saw, cut to the limit on both sides first; then, cut the remaining stock with a hand crosscut saw or a band saw.

A

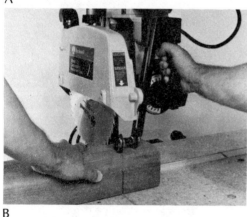

B

Fig. 3-9: Making a crosscut through a thick workpiece in two passes.

Crosscutting Small Pieces. Because of the movement involved in the crosscutting action (Fig. 3-2A), when the teeth of the blade engage the stock they actually push the workpiece down and back against the fence. For this reason, it is generally not necessary to solidly clamp or grip a small workpiece when crosscutting it. A small piece of stock can be held in place against the fence with a fairly light touch. On really small pieces, it is best to nail or clamp the work to the table. Remember, when work is held by hand, keep your hand in position until the cuttinghead has been returned to its starting position behind the fence. The other hand should remain on the yoke handle until the blade comes to a rest.

When the stock that is to be cut does not have a straight edge or end long enough to rest firmly against the table fence, and it is large enough to be reached, clamp it with a C-clamp to the front or on one side of the worktable, to keep it from shifting while sawing. A corner removed from the stop block against the fence will eliminate the sawdust build-up problem.

Do not attempt to hold a small or oddly-shaped workpiece freehand. This is dangerous. Instead, you can nail the workpiece to a larger, straight-edged scrap board, that will rest flat against the fence. Or, use a homemade jig, like the one shown in Fig. 3-10. The jig must be placed so that it will hold the workpiece firmly,

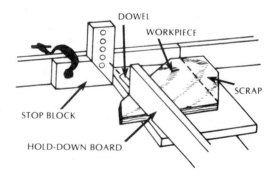

Fig. 3-10: A jig for holding small or oddly-shaped workpieces when crosscutting.

until the carriage has been returned to the back of the arm and the blade is behind the table fence.

Gang or Duplicate Crosscutting. As many workpieces as will fit on the worktable can be crosscut in one operation, if they are all held firmly on the worktable and against the guide fence. However, when four or more workpieces are to be cut at once, some may slide during the cut, binding the blade and ruining the work. If all of the workpieces are to be cut to the same length, you can ensure a straight, accurate cut by clamping a straight, flat piece of scrapboard to the end of the table and butting the ends of the workpieces against it, as shown in Fig. 3-11. Remember to hold the stock on the same side as the stop block.

Fig. 3-11: Using a stop block for gang cross-cutting.

Duplicate cut-off pieces can be made by clamping a stop block to the fence in the same manner as described for oversize stock. To locate the block, measure the desired size of the cut-off workpieces from the crosscut groove in the fence. Each workpiece need only be butted against the stop block (Fig. 3-12) and an equal cut-off length will be achieved. However, make certain that sawdust does not pile up against the stop, for the accumulation can throw off the accuracy of your setting.

To avoid the use of C-clamps and adjustable hand screws when cutting duplicate pieces, an adjustable stop block such as the one shown in Fig. 3-13 is ideal. When the front metal plate is pressed, the clamp is released and can be adjusted at any point along the fence. It works on either side of the saw blade.

As shown in Fig. 3-14, the main block is made of hard wood such as maple, beech, or birch. All metal parts are made from 16 gauge cold rolled steel bent to shape, as indicated in the line drawing. The metal spacer strips "D" are 1/64 inch thicker. Piece "B" is free to slide under the top piece "C". Two 13/32 inch holes, 1 inch deep and 1 9/16 inches apart, are bored in the wood block "A" for the 3/8 inch compression springs. The two metal spacers "D" and hand finger support "C" are screw fastened to the hardwood block "A" with four No. 8 x 7/8 inch flat head sheet metal screws as shown in the line drawing. A strip of coarse aluminum oxide abrasive

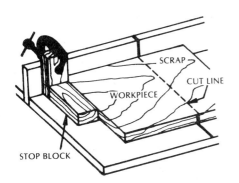

Fig. 3-12: Making duplicate cut-off pieces.

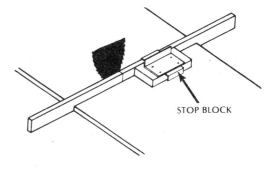

Fig. 3-13: An adjustable stop block.

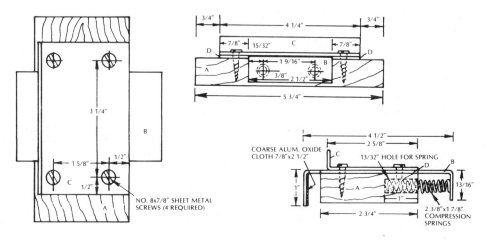

Fig. 3-14: Dimensions for an adjustable stop block.

cloth, 7/8 inch wide by 2 1/2 inches long, is glued to the inside surface of the bent section "B" with shellac or rubber cement. This aluminum oxide abrasive cloth keeps the clamp from sliding along the fence when the stock to be cut is held against the clamp.

Stopped Cuts and Slots. A block of wood clamped to the radial arm with a small C-clamp will prevent unnecessary travel of the cuttinghead on the track or radial arm. This is especially handy when performing repetitive operations. Clamp the wood stop block to the right side of the radial arm at a position which will stop the cuttinghead travel as soon as the saw blade cuts through the workpiece (Fig. 3-15).

A wood stop block clamped to the radial arm also makes it easy to cut through a workpiece, up to a finish line short of the complete cut. But, when using a stop block in this manner, be sure to wait for the blade to completely stop, before disengaging it from the workpiece.

Crosscut slots can be sawed with a radial saw by both starting and stopping the cut short of the workpiece sides. To do this, first lower the blade 1/32 to 1/16 inch below the worktable top; then elevate the blade to just clear the workpiece top, counting the number of elevation crank revolutions. Once the workpiece is posi-

Fig. 3-15: Using a wood stop block on the radial arm, to stop the cuttinghead travel.

tioned on the table top, clamp it firmly in place. Locate the cuttinghead in the desired position at the beginning of the cut, and lock it in place by tightening the carriage clamp knob. Then, turn the saw ON, and slowly lower the saw blade by the same number of elevation crank revolutions required to raise it. Loosen the carriage clamp knob while holding the cuttinghead stationary with the yoke handle, then complete the operation in the same manner as for a stopped cut.

Dado Cutting. A dado is a slot cut across the grain or through the width of a workpiece (Fig. 3-16). With the cuttinghead in the crosscut position, lower the blade to the desired depth of the dado. Start at one end of the dado and pull the blade through the workpiece. After returning the cuttinghead to the column, move the workpiece 1/8 inch and bring the blade forward again. Continue this repeat pass operation until the desired width of the dado is obtained.

Horizontal Crosscutting. Horizontal crosscutting, end crosscutting, or simply end cutting, as this operation is also known, is used for cutting across the end of any size workpiece (Fig. 3-17). To locate the

Fig. 3-16: Cutting a cross dado with a saw blade.

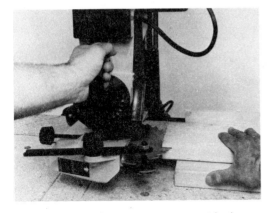

Fig. 3-17: Horizontal crosscutting with the radial saw.

blade in the horizontal position, raise the radial arm on the column by turning the elevating crank until the bottom of the blade is approximately 3 inches above the table top. With the saw in the crosscut position, pull it to the front end of the radial arm. Hold the top of the blade guard in your left hand, and release the bevel clamp handle. Swing the motor and blade into the 90-degree horizontal position, (it will seat itself at precisely 90 degrees), the blade being parallel to the worktable, and lock the bevel clamp handle. The cuttinghead will now be in a vertical position, putting the blade in a horizontal position. Adjust the dust elbow on the blade guard, making it parallel with the worktable and directed away from the operator. Push the carriage back towards the column in the normal vertical crosscutting starting position.

Place the workpiece to be cut against the fence, and lower the blade to the plane where the end cut is to be made. The depth of the cut will be determined by the location of the workpiece, in respect to the blade. Waste blocks or an auxiliary table should be placed under the workpiece, when necessary, to make sure the proper plane and depth of cut are achieved. The saw blade elevation can usually be aligned by eye with the height of the desired cut.

Turn the saw ON, and with the cuttinghead behind the fence, pull it through the workpiece in the same manner as when crosscutting. If you wish to increase the width of the end cut, push the saw back against the column and raise or lower the arm a full turn. Bring the saw forward again and then return it to the column. Repeat this procedure until the desired width of the end cut is obtained.

When horizontal crosscutting thin stock, it will be necessary to build an auxiliary table and fence (as shown in Fig. 3-18), because the thickness of the blade guard will not allow the blade to be lowered more than 1 1/4 inches above the stationary worktable top. The auxiliary worktable is installed in place of the standard table

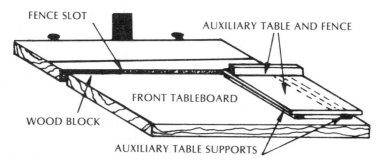

FENCE SLOT

AUXILIARY TABLE AND FENCE

FRONT TABLEBOARD

WOOD BLOCK

AUXILIARY TABLE SUPPORTS

Fig. 3-18: An auxiliary table and fence for horizontal crosscutting thin stock.

fence. To do this, release the two table board clamps, lift the table fence out, slide in the auxiliary worktable, and retighten the table board clamps. The workpiece will now be located against the auxiliary-table fence and can be cut as previously described.

A typical horizontal sawing operation is the cutting of end rabbets in two passes. To accomplish this, lay the workpiece flat against the table fence and make a crosscut along the end with the blade in the horizontal position (Fig. 3-19A). Make the second cut to the depth of the rabbet with the saw in the standard crosscut position (Fig. 3-19B).

Rabbets can also be sawed with the blade in either the vertical or horizontal position using the repeat pass technique described for cutting dadoes. For example, with the blade in the horizontal position, set the depth of the rabbet and start cutting at the top edge of the board. Then lower the blade a full turn at a time until the desired rabbet is obtained.

Bevel Crosscutting. Bevel crosscutting is similar to straight crosscutting, but the saw is tilted to the desired bevel angle (Fig. 3-20). With the cuttinghead back against the column, elevate the radial arm so that the blade will clear the table top when swiveling the cuttinghead in the yoke. Pull the carriage to the front end of the arm. To tilt the cuttinghead, place your left hand on top of the blade guard, and release the bevel clamp handle. Manually, push the

cuttinghead out of the seated 90 degree position and move it to the degree desired by using the bevel angle scale and pointer. Then lock the bevel clamp handle. Turn

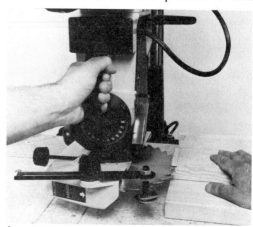

A

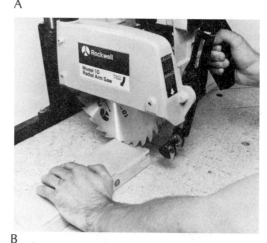

B

Fig. 3-19: Cutting an end rabbet with a saw blade, making, (A) a horizontal crosscut first, and then (B) a straight vertical crosscut.

38

Fig. 3-20: Setting the cuttinghead for a bevel crosscut.

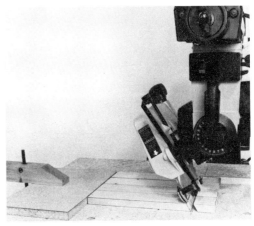

Fig. 3-21: Making a gang bevel crosscut.

the elevating crank down until the saw-blade teeth cut about 1/32 to 1/16 inch into the table top, as when crosscutting. Push the carriage back along the radial arm to the column. If a common 45-degree bevel is desired, simply let the cuttinghead seat itself in the 45-degree slot. Then lock the bevel clamp handle. In both cases, if not previously done, the table fence will need to be cut, by raising the blade to clear the fence, returning the cuttinghead to the column, lowering the blade to the previous setting, turning the saw ON, and cutting through the table fence.

Place the stock on the worktable top against the table fence. Adjust the blade guard and keep your fingers clear, the same as when crosscutting. To make the bevel cutoff on the left side, hold the stock with the left hand and pull the cuttinghead with the right hand by using the yoke handle. When cutting on the right side, reverse the way you hold your hands.

To cross bevel several similar pieces, place them together as you would for a simple gang crosscut. Hold them firmly together in place and pull the saw blade across the entire gang (Fig. 3-21).

MITERING

Mitering is the same basic procedure as crosscutting, except that the travel arm is revolved on a horizontal plane to any other angle besides a straight 90 degrees. It is used extensively in the workshop to make various frames, to fit moldings, and for many other functional and decorative purposes. In construction, it is the method used to produce rafters, angle beams, and stairway stringers. More than any other tool, the radial saw is exceptionally suited to make mitering easy and accurate for the beginner as well as the skilled artisan.

Right-hand Miter. Make sure the cuttinghead is in back of the table fence and against the column. With the left hand, release the radial arm clamp knob. With the right hand on the travel arm, swing it to the right to the angle desired by following the miter scale. Then lock the radial arm clamp knob. The popular 45-degree miter cut is set quickly with the radial arm index knob, which automatically seats the arm in the 45-degree positions. Next, place the workpiece flat on the worktable top, and firmly against the table fence. Adjust the blade guard parallel to the bottom of the motor; adjust the anti-kickback fingers down to 1/8 inch above the workpiece, hold the workpiece with the left hand, and pull the saw through the material with the right hand (Fig. 3-22). Return the saw to its original position at the rear of the fence before removing the workpiece from the

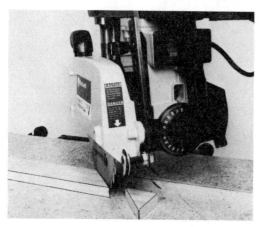

Fig. 3-22: Making a right-hand miter cut at 45 degrees.

Fig. 3-23: Making a left-hand miter cut at 45 degrees.

table top. To avoid scoring the worktable too much when cutting miters at an angle other than 45 degrees, place a piece of scrap material on the table top and engage the blade in the scrap.

When the stock is flat, it is easy to make miter cuts at each end of the workpiece. The work can be flipped for alternate cuts. But, when decorative moldings are to be cut, it is usually necessary to make left-hand miters as well as right.

Left-hand Miter. Move the travel arm to the left to the desired angle in the manner described for a right-hand miter. To achieve the maximum capacity for a left-hand miter, move the table fence to the rear of the rear table board. To make this adjustment, release the two table board clamps holding the table boards, and move the table fence back.

board clamps. Place the workpiece flat on the table top and firmly against the fence. Adjust the blade guard and anti-kickback fingers, the same as you would for a right-hand miter cut. With the right hand holding the stock, pull the blade through the workpiece with the left hand (Fig. 3-23). Then return the cuttinghead to its original position.

In mitering operations there is always a tendency for the work to creep laterally away from the feed. This is especially true

when making cuts at a wide angle. It is advisable, therefore, when mitering, to hold the material very firmly and to draw the blade through slowly—allowing it to cut through cleanly without "walking." Many craftshop owners make use of an auxiliary guide fence with "anchor points" when mitering. This is simply a fence with screw points protruding, to aid in gripping the stock and to prevent lateral movement (Fig 3-24). You can make one readily and

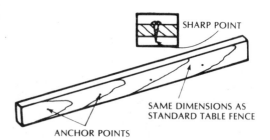

Fig. 3-24: An auxiliary guide fence with "anchor points" to prevent creeping when mitering.

use it whenever you wish to be sure of very accurate mitering work. When the miter cut makes an angle of less than 30 degrees with the fence, the work should be clamped or a stop block should be used.

When duplicating mitered-end pieces, a stop similar to the one shown in Fig. 3-25 is most helpful. It will help prevent the workpiece from creeping along the fence

Fig. 3-25: Using a stop for duplicating mitered-end pieces.

Fig. 3-27: Another V-shaped mitering jig, which can also be used on a table saw.

to spoil the cut. The operation calls for cutting the parts to the correct length first, using the simple straight cut-off. After the stock has been mitered at one end, each piece is flopped end-over-end for its second cut at the same miter setting and against the stop.

V-shaped mitering jigs such as shown in Figs. 3-26 and 3-27, position the work at the correct angle and let you do the mitering job as if it were a simple crosscut. As a result, work placement, assured by the jigs, establishes the accuracy of the cut.

When miter crosscutting wide boards, you can rotate the board 180 degrees to make the second pass at the same miter angle, or you can flop the board. When

flopping the boards, after repositioning the stock, reset the miter scale to the same angle, but at the other side of 0 degrees by pivoting the radial arm. Then make the second cut.

Bevel Mitering. A bevel miter, sometimes called a compound angle cut, or double miter, is a combination of a miter and a bevel (Fig. 3-28). Bevel miters are usually used to build structures with sloping sides, such as shadow box picture frames, tilting sided boxes, or even hip-roof rafters. The chart on page 68 shows saw settings at 5-degree intervals, for obtaining various compound angles.

To set the saw up for a bevel miter, first set the cuttinghead to the angle desired by

Fig. 3-26: A V-shaped mitering jig.

Fig. 3-28: A workpiece with a bevel miter or compound angle at one end.

A

B

Fig. 3-29: *Using the first-cut piece as a template when cutting pieces of similar length consecutively from one long board.*

following the bevel scale and then locking the bevel clamp handle. Release the radial arm index knob and the radial arm clamp knob and swing the radial arm into the desired miter position, following the same routine as for miter cuts. To make the cut, follow the normal operating routine described under bevel crosscutting.

Frequently, when cutting pieces of similar length consecutively from one long board (Fig. 3-29A), it is possible to employ the first piece cut as a template for marking the succeeding cuts. Rotate the first piece and place it as shown in Fig. 3-29B. Use a very sharp pencil when marking the cut line. On the next cut, the kerf will be on the waste side and should just remove the pencil line. By rotating the stock as just described, all cuts can be made in the right miter position.

More information on making compound angle cuts can be found in Chapter 5.

RIPPING ACTION

Straight ripping is done with the saw blade parallel to the table fence, while feeding the workpiece into the saw blade. You can rip from either the left or right side of the machine. The feed of the workpiece into the saw depends on the rotation of the saw blade. When ripping from the right side of the table, known as in-ripping, the yoke and cuttinghead must be swiveled 90 degrees so that the blade is between the motor and the column. To rip from the left side of the machine, called out-ripping, swivel the yoke and cuttinghead 90 degrees so that the motor is between the blade and the column. The yoke and cuttinghead automatically seat in either position as they swivel on the carriage.

Figure 3-30 shows the maximum in-rip and out-rip blade positions of a typical 10-inch radial saw with the table fence in the normal and rear-most positions. The maximum in-rip with the table fence in the normal position is about 7 inches. The in-rip position should be used as much as possible, because it places the blade away from the operator. In-ripping is always done from the right-hand side of the table, feeding the workpiece toward the left, using the right hand to feed. When out-ripping, the feed is from the left-hand side

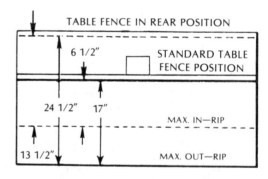

Fig. 3-30: *Maximum in-rip and out-rip blade positions of a typical 10-inch radial saw.*

Fig. 3-31: Setting the in-rip scale with the table fence in its rearmost position.

Fig. 3-32: When ripping, lower the front of the blade guard to within 1/8 inch of the workpiece, adjust the anti-kickback fingers, and be sure the splitter is aligned with the blade.

of the table toward the right, using the left hand to feed, which is slightly harder to do for most operators. Remember, the workpiece is always fed into the blade against the direction in which the teeth at the bottom of the blade are moving as they cut into the workpiece. From the front of the table, the blade in an in-rip position revolves counterclockwise; with the blade in an out-rip position, it revolves clockwise.

In-ripping. To set your saw in the in-rip position, pull the cuttinghead to the front end of the radial arm. Release the yoke clamp handle. Swivel the yoke clockwise 90 degrees from the crosscut position. A swivel location pin will snap into position automatically. Tighten the yoke clamp handle.

The in-rip scale or rule on the right side of the arm (facing the front of the saw) is set with the table fence in its rearmost position. With the saw blade against the fence, the pointer on the carriage should read zero on the top side of the scale marked "in-rip" (Fig. 3-31). This rule and pointer can be off as much as 1/16 inch because of differences in the types of saw blades. Some saw blades have set teeth, while

others may be hollow ground with no set in the teeth. To adjust the scale to the proper setting, follow the instructions given in Chapter 2. Set the saw to the desired width of rip by using the pointer and scale. Then tighten the carriage clamp knob to hold the saw in position. To ensure precision work, the distance between the blade and the fence can be set using a rule or tape measure.

Before ripping, adjust the guard, splitter, and anti-kickback fingers to the proper position, as described here and as shown in Fig. 3-32. Lay the workpiece on the worktable top, close to the blade guard. Release the blade guard clamp knob holding the blade guard to the motor and rotate the guard down to approximately 1/8 inch above the top surface of the workpiece you are ripping. Retighten the clamp knob. On the opposite end of the blade guard is the anti-kickback assembly. Release the clamp knob for the anti-kickback device and adjust the holding arm until the fingers are 1/8 inch below the top surface of the workpiece you are going to rip. Retighten the anti-kickback device clamp knob. On the top side of the blade guard is the dust spout. Adjust it until the spout is turned toward the back of the machine to carry the dust away from you.

With the saw set in the in-rip position, feed the workpiece into the saw from the

Fig. 3-33: Use a right-hand feed when in-ripping, and use the left hand to guide the work.

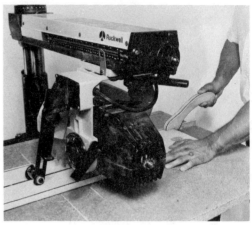

Fig. 3-35: Using a push stick for ripping.

right side of the machine. With the left hand approximately 6 inches in back of the blade guard, hold the workpiece down and back against the table fence. Now, with the right hand, move the workpiece into the saw by standing on the front right side of the machine and let the workpiece slide through your left hand (Fig. 3-33). When the right hand meets the left hand, continue the balance of the rip by using a push stick similar to the one shown in Fig. 3-34. Hold the push stick against the table fence and against the end of the workpiece you are ripping (Fig. 3-35) and continue on through until the workpiece clears the saw blade on the opposite side by 2 inches. Pull

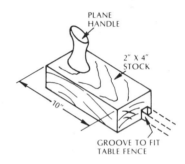

Fig. 3-36: A push stick especially designed for in-ripping narrow work.

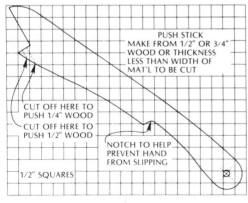

Fig. 3-34: A push stick for ripping operations.

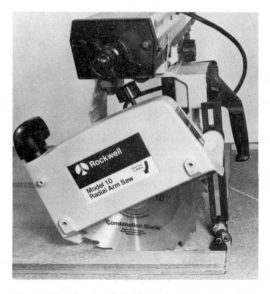

Fig. 3-37: The feed is from the left side of the machine for out-ripping.

the push stick straight back.

The push stick shown in Fig. 3-36 is ideal for narrow work since it is designed to straddle the fence so it cannot slip. The long handle permits workpieces to be pushed past the blade without endangering the hands.

Out-ripping. When ripping wide materials such as panel boards, you should swivel the saw 90 degrees counterclockwise from the crosscut position to the out-rip position. With the saw set to the out-rip position, use the out-rip scale on the left side of the radial saw (facing the front of the saw). This scale can be used to a capacity of about 24 inches with the table fence in its rear-most position. Make the blade guard and anti-kickback device adjustments as previously described for in-ripping. When the saw is set for out-ripping the workpiece must be fed into the saw from the left side of the machine (Fig. 3-37).

Ripping a Narrow Workpiece or a Workpiece with a Narrow Width-of-rip. With a workpiece 3 inches or less in width, put the saw in the in-rip position and use a push stick as previously described. The push stick must be long enough to pass beneath the end of the blade guard, while pushing the workpiece past the blade to finish the rip. However, the operator's hand should never approach closer than 8 inches to the blade.

If the distance from the fence to the blade is less than 6 inches but more than 1/4 inch, a push stick must be used, feeding the workpiece along the table fence in the

Fig. 3-38: Using a featherboard to keep the workpiece against the fence when ripping.

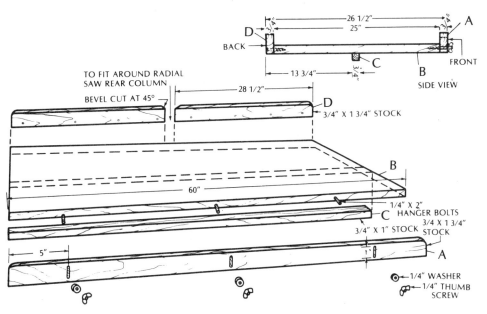

Fig. 3-39: An auxiliary worktable for ripping long, narrow strips.

usual manner. If the workpiece is long enough to extend over the in-feed end of the table at the start of the rip, the work should be fed into the blade by hand, until the rear end of the workpiece is no less than 12 inches from the blade, when the operator should switch to a push stick to finish.

When ripping thin stock, the flexibility of wood and the tendency of the saw blade to lift the workpiece, make it difficult to safely hold the work against the fence. If this should be the case, use one or more feather- or fingerboards (Fig. 3-38).

For additional support when ripping long stock on the radial saw, and especially for very narrow strips, the table illustrated in Fig. 3-39 is helpful. The front guide strip "A" is easily lowered by simply loosening the three 1/4 inch thumb screws when ripping wide stock. Strip "C" which is glued and nailed to the underside of the auxiliary table, fits into the guide fence position in the standard worktable. Back strips "D" are used as a permanent back fence. Top piece "B" is made of 3/4 inch plywood; all other parts are made of solid stock. Apply three coats of polyurethane finish.

The pushing device shown in Fig. 3-40 is most helpful when working with the ripping table. A solid block of 2 x 4 hardwood with a hand grip, cut to shape as indicated in the drawing, and a piece of 1/8-inch hardboard glued and nailed to the rabbeted edge will complete the project. Smooth all sharp corners and apply a coat of polyurethane finish.

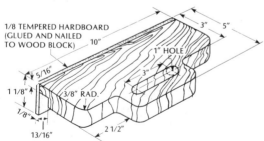

Fig. 3-40: A pushing device that fits over the table fence.

Ripping a Long Workpiece. When ripping a long workpiece, it is important to support the extended end or ends, and to prevent the workpiece from rocking back and forth. A sawhorse can be used as a support where it is needed, much as it is used for supporting the ends of a long workpiece when crosscutting. Even better than a saw horse, is a height adjustable roller support (Fig. 3-41) or a long board, level with the table and supported on its outboard end. Regardless of the device used to support the workpiece, it should be stable and level with the surface of the worktable.

Fig. 3-41: A height adjustable roller support for ripping long work.

Also, to prevent the kerf (line already cut) in a long workpiece from closing, which will cause the workpiece to bind on the blade, it (the kerf) should be wedged open as soon as it begins to close (Fig. 3-42). The splitter will automatically perform this task, if properly adjusted.

Ripping Stock with an Unstraight Edge. Never rip a workpiece by guiding an unstraight edge along the table fence. Any variation from a straight-line feed will bind

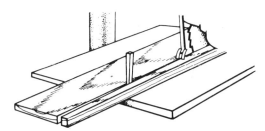

Fig. 3-42: Wedging the kerf open on a long workpiece, to prevent the wood from binding on the blade.

the blade and cause kickback. If you have a workpiece to be ripped, which has an unstraight edge, either nail a straightedge to the workpiece to act as a guiding edge, or clamp a straightedged piece of scrapboard to the outer bottom side of the workpiece to act as a fence along the front edge of the front table board (Fig. 3-43).

Stopped Rip Cuts and Slots. To rip through a piece of stock up to a finish line short of the end of the workpiece is simply done by clamping a stop to the table fence or to the worktable to halt the work's movement (Fig. 3-44). Remember to let the saw blade come to a complete stop before removing the workpiece from the table.

To cut rip slots in a workpiece, first lower the saw blade to 1/32 to 1/16 inch below the top table and then elevate it to just clear the workpiece top, counting the number of elevating crank turns. Position

the workpiece on the table top, clamping it firmly in place. With the cuttinghead locked into the proper starting position, start the motor and slowly lower the blade by the same number of elevating crank turns required to raise it. Turn off the motor, and when it comes to a complete stop, unclamp the workpiece and adjust the guard, splitter, and anti-kickback fingers as required for ripping. Holding the workpiece securely, start the motor and complete the sawing operation as for a stopped cut.

Resawing. Resawing is the operation of ripping a thick board to make two thinner ones. If the work does not exceed the capacity of the saw, the cut can be treated as a regular ripping operation. However, it is often necessary to cut part of the way through the workpiece (Fig. 3-45A), invert it, and complete the cut (Fig. 3-45B).

When resawing, the blade can be placed in either the in-rip or out-rip position. The blade should be set just a little more than half the width of the workpiece when the workpiece is *less* in width than twice the capacity of the saw. For example, let us assume that it is necessary to resaw a board 4 inches wide by 2 inches thick into two boards. Taking into consideration that the capacity of the particular saw blade is 2 1/2 inches, about 1 1/2 inches are left for the

Fig. 3-43: Using a scrapboard clamped to the outer bottom side of a workpiece to act as a fence along the front edge of the worktable.

Fig. 3-44: Using a stop block clamped to the table fence, to make a stopped rip.

A

B

Fig. 3-45: To resaw a wide board, it is often necessary to: (A) cut part of the way through, (B) invert the workpiece, and complete the cut.

lar to horizontal crosscutting except that the cut is made on the edge or side of the stock rather than on the end. To place the saw blade in the horizontal rip position, first locate the saw for out-ripping and then turn it to 90 degrees on the bevel scale as described in horizontal crosscutting.

Place the workpiece against the table fence, either standard or auxiliary, depending on its thickness, and locate the height and depth of the cut. A piece of 3/4-inch plywood can be used as an auxiliary table, as shown in Fig. 3-47. It is pushed along with the stock when the cut is made. The yoke clamp handle and the carriage clamp knob are tightened, and the workpiece is pushed past the blade the same way as when straight ripping. If a groove is

second cut. However, when the depth of the board to be resawed is greater than twice the capacity of the machine, make the cuts as deep as possible from each edge. Then finish the ripping by hand or with a band saw. Never attempt to resaw a board less than 1 inch thick on a radial saw.

An important point to bear in mind when resawing, is to keep the same surface of the workpiece against an auxiliary table fence which is at least three-quarters as high as the stock for both cuts. Reverse the workpiece end-to-end, never side-to-side, when making the second cut since this will not change the tool setup. It is also a good idea to place a small wedge in each end of the first cut to hold it open when making the second cut (Fig. 3-46).

Horizontal Ripping. Horizontal ripping or edge cutting, as it is also known, is simi-

Fig. 3-46: Using wedges to hold open the kerf when resawing.

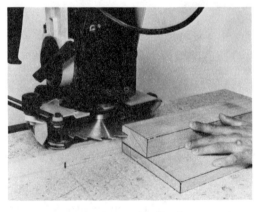

Fig. 3-47: An auxiliary table for horizontal ripping.

desired, the radial arm may be raised or lowered a full turn at a time and the operation repeated until the proper width is obtained.

Grooving and Rabbeting. A groove of any width can be made by using the repeat-pass technique described earlier in this chapter for dado cutting. It is a good idea to make the two outside groove cuts, locating them at the exact width and depth desired. After these cuts have been made, make as many passes as necessary, to clean out the center area (Fig. 3-48).

While rabbets can be cut by the repeat-pass method, another method of rabbeting the edge of a board is to make two saw cuts at right angles to each other. Lay out the rabbet on the end of the board and mark it off. When the length of the board is within the crosscut capacity of the saw, the first cut is made with the blade in the normal crosscut position and the board is placed on edge, one end against the fence, and clamped to the worktable using clamp blocks (Fig. 3-49A). The second cut is a normal crosscut operation.

Longer boards must be ripped to make the rabbet. Be sure the fence is at least one-half as high as the workpiece. The first ripping cut is made with the workpiece on edge against the fence. The second ripping cut is made with the workpiece flat on the table. Be sure the waste portion is not a-

A

B

Fig. 3-49: Two different ways of cutting rabbets using two saw cuts, rather than the repeat-pass method.

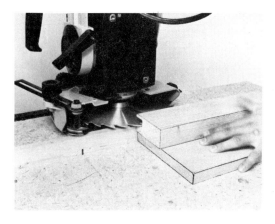

Fig. 3-48: Cutting a groove with a saw blade.

gainst the fence, because when cutting in the in-rip position, a strip of wood between the table fence and the uncut portion of the workpiece, that is called an arrow, will be cut loose and may shoot back at the operator with considerable force unless the piece is held by a push stick. If this cut is made in the in-rip position with the rabbet away from the table fence (Fig. 3-49B) or in the out-rip position, the piece will simply fall off with no kickback to worry about.

Bevel Ripping. Bevel ripping is simply ripping with the cuttinghead tilted for angle cuts (Fig. 3-50). With the saw swiveled to the rip position (either in- or out-rip), elevate the column by rotating the elevating crank, and then release the bevel clamp handle. Turn the cuttinghead within

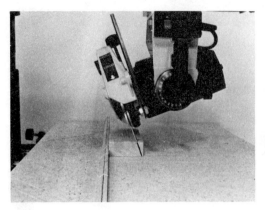

Fig. 3-50: The cuttinghead is tilted for bevel ripping.

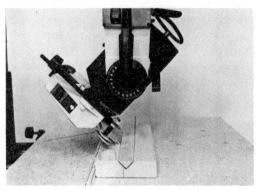

Fig. 3-52: Cutting a V-groove in the center of a workpiece, without resetting the blade for the second cut.

the yoke to the desired angle. If the 45-degree position is desired, set it, and securely clamp the cuttinghead in place with the bevel clamp handle. Adjust the blade guard on the in-feed end to within 1/8 inch of the workpiece. Push the work through as previously described for normal in- or out-rip sawing. But remember, the in- and out-rip scales indicate the width of the cut for the vertical blade position only. When setting the width for a bevel cut, you must use your eye and/or a layout mark (Fig. 3-51).

Cutting V-grooves. As you will see in succeeding chapters, one of the most useful special devices or jigs you can make is a V-block. It can easily be made by bevel-ripping. After placing the blade in the 45-degree position, lower the blade to the desired depth of the V in the stock. Locate the cuttinghead and lock the carriage clamp knob. Turn the saw ON and pass the

workpiece past the blade as previously described. When the V is in the center of the workpiece, reverse the stock, and pass it through the blade again (Fig. 3-52). When it is located elsewhere, the blade must be reset to mate the second cut with the first cut.

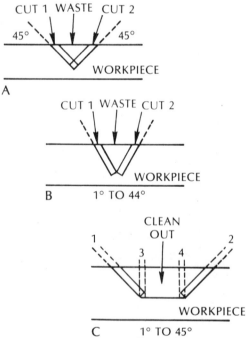

Fig. 3-53: (A) To get a perfect V at the bottom of the groove, it is necessary to make two 45 degree cuts; (B) if any other bevel angle is used, there will be a slight hump at the bottom; (C) technique for cutting a flat-bottom V-groove.

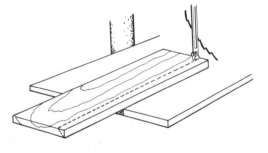

Fig. 3-51: Layout marks for a bevel rip.

50

Many interesting decorative panel treatments can be made by combining various bevel cuts. A perfect V at the bottom, as previously described, can be made by having the two 45-degree cuts meet as illustrated in Fig. 3-53A. If any other bevel angle is employed, there will be a slight hump in the middle (Fig. 3-53B). A flat-bottom V can be formed by making the two outside cuts shown in Fig. 3-53C, and then removing the center section in the same manner as for rip grooving. Regardless of the notched shape desired, it is best to draw the shape on the end of the workpiece and make all saw set-ups accordingly.

The crosscut action can also be used to cut V-blocks and decorative grooves (Fig. 3-54).

Chamfering. Chamfering, also known as bevel edge-cutting, is simply making bevel cuts along the top edges of the stock (Fig. 3-55A). Set the saw in the rip-bevel position at an angle of 20 to 45 degrees. Position the blade so that it overhangs the workpiece by the desired width of the cut, and lock it in place with the carriage clamp knob. Push the workpiece along the table fence and through the path of the blade. If both edges are to be chamfered, reverse the workpiece and cut along the other top edge in the same manner.

Narrow workpieces can be pushed into the blade in the normal ripping manner,

A

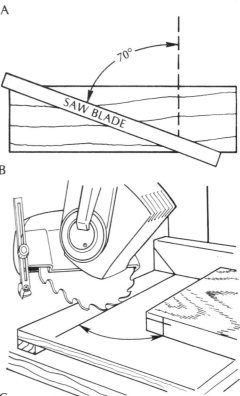

B

C

Fig. 3-55: (A) A typical chamfer cut; (B) the maximum angle and position at which a chamfer can be cut with the workpiece flat on the worktable; (C) marking the bevel angle for a chamfer cut.

but must be pulled past the blade, because the tilted blade guard does not leave enough clearance for a push stick next to the fence.

Cross-chamfering is achieved by placing

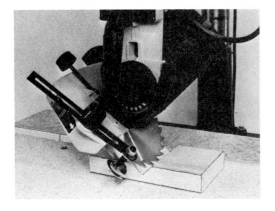

Fig. 3-54: Crosscutting a V-groove.

the blade in the crosscut-bevel position at the desired angle. Position the blade so that it overhangs the stock by the desired width (as for a rip-chamfer). Then pull the cuttinghead through in the prescribed crosscut method.

Figure 3-55B shows the maximum angle and position at which a chamfer can be cut with the workpiece flat on the worktable. An auxiliary table must be used if the workpiece has to be elevated. To position the workpiece, mark the line of the desired bevel on its edge as shown in Fig. 3-55C; measure the bevel angle, and set the cuttinghead to the angle on the bevel angle scale; then, lower the blade to groove the auxiliary worktable. Align the workpiece mark with this groove to make the cut.

The octagon shape required for lathe spindle work can be cut in the same manner as described for chamfer cutting.

Bevel Rabbeting. The two-cut bevel rabbet, a shape that is handy when you wish to join two pieces at an angle, is cut in the same manner except that the first cut is a horizontal bevel rip (Fig. 3-56A), followed by a straight vertical rip cut (Fig. 3-56B). An auxiliary table is generally used for this operation.

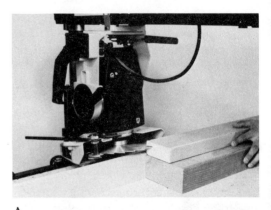

A

B

Fig. 3-56: Making a bevel rabbet with two cuts: (A) a horizontal bevel rip; (B) a straight vertical rip.

Chapter 4

BASIC USE OF THE DADO HEAD

The dado head is one of the most useful radial saw accessories you can own. The primary function of a dado head is to cut grooves, dadoes, and rabbets. While these cuts can be made by either two-cut or repeat pass methods as described in the previous chapter, the purchase of a dado head is a wise choice if such cuts are needed often, because the dado head facilitates easier and faster production.

Actually, the dado head is basically a thick sawing blade. But remember, it is used to remove stock from a given area, rather than for cutting through the stock. Nevertheless, it is used much the same as a regular blade. Much of the work done with a dado head is preparing material for a wide variety of joints. However, this accessory can perform tasks other than the simple cutting of dadoes, grooves, and rabbets.

BASIC DADO OPERATIONS

A description of the various types of dado heads was given in Chapter 1. For dado-head mounting and width-spacing (or adjustable-dado setting) instructions, refer to the instructions furnished with the dado head. When using the standard type of dado head, make sure that the chippers are heavily swaged and arranged so that this heavy portion falls in the gullets of the outside blades, as shown in Fig. 4-1A. The blade and chipper overlap as shown in Fig. 4-1B, (a) being the outside blade, (b) the inside chipper, and (c) a paper washer or washers which can be used as needed to control the exact width of the groove, dado, or rabbet. A 1/4 inch groove or dado is cut by using the two outside blades ar-

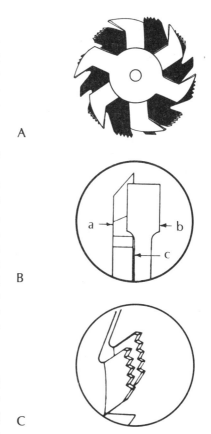

A

B

C

Fig. 4-1: Standard dado head and adjustments.

ranged as shown in Fig. 4-1C. The teeth of the blades should be positioned so that the raker on one blade is beside the cutting teeth on the other blade.

Mounting the Dado Head. The dado head—either the adjustable or the standard type—is fitted and secured to the arbor (primary motor shaft) in the same manner as a regular saw blade (Fig. 4-2). For dado cuts up to 1/2 inch, place the 3/8-inch arbor collar on the shaft first, with its re-

*NOTE: *To clearly illustrate certain procedures described in this chapter, the blade guard and other safety devices have been removed. To safely operate the radial saw, the guards and other safety devices must always be utilized.*

53

Fig. 4-2: Securing the dado head to the motor shaft saw arbor.

cessed side against the dado head; the dado-head assembly next; then the 1/4-inch arbor collar, with its recessed side against the dado head; and finally, tighten the arbor nut with the two wrenches supplied with the saw. For cuts of more than 1/2 inch, omit the 1/4-inch arbor collar. When using the full dado head, first put on the 1/4 arbor collar, the 13/16-inch dado head, and then the arbor nut. Mount the blade guard over the dado head, adjust the guard for the work to be done, and tighten the blade guard clamp knob. Remember to use all of the normal protective devices when doing normal vertical dado head operations.

In a dado head there is quite a mass of metal revolving at a fairly high speed; if it is not running true it will vibrate noticeably. This can be avoided by staggering the teeth properly and tightening the dado to the full extent.

The width of the cut is determined by adjusting the dado head to the desired size, but never use the chipper blades without the two outside saw blades. For example, to cut a dado 1/2 inch wide, use the two outside saw blades, each 1/8 inch in width, plus a single 1/4-inch or two 1/8-inch chippers. Actually, any width dado head can be used (the size being limited only by the length of the motor shaft arbor). However, most dado-head sets have enough blades to make cuts only up to 13/16 inch wide.

When the width of the finished cut is to be more than 13/16 inch, set up the dado head to a little more than half the required width of the cut and make two successive cuts. Each cut must overlap a bit at the center. If the width of the dado is to be more than twice the capacity of the dado head, set it for a little more than one-third of the width and make three overlapping cuts. It is preferable to make the two outside cuts first, carefully aligning each cut with its respective side of the dado (Fig. 4-3). The center cuts can then be made without particular attention to the alignment.

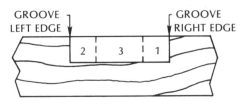

Fig. 4-3: The two outside cuts of a wide dado are made first.

Simply have each cut overlap the adjacent one(s) by at least 1/16 inch. The depth of cut is controlled by raising or lowering the cuttinghead by turning the elevating crank.

The dado head may be pulled or lowered into the workpiece, or the workpiece can be pushed into the dado head. When dadoing, use a slightly slower than normal feed to insure smooth work. Also, there is a tendency for the work to "creep" when dadoing (removing) material of any substantial width; therefore, it is recommended that the workpiece be securely clamped to the table before beginning the cut.

CUTTING DADOES

The operation for a simple cross dado is essentially the same as for crosscutting. With the cuttinghead in the crosscut position, elevate or lower the radial arm with the elevating crank until the depth of the dado is reached. Then pull the cuttinghead past the stock, which must be held tightly against the table fence (Fig. 4-4). A mechanical stop block arrangement such as described in the previous chapter on crosscutting, may be used when more than one piece is to be dadoed.

A

B

Fig. 4-5: Determining the depth of a dado: (A) lowering the dado head until it barely touches the workpiece; (B) pushing the cuttinghead towards the column and lowering the dado head to the desired depth of cut, using the elevating crank.

Fig. 4-4: A typical cross dado operation.

To locate a dado, use a rule to measure from one end of the workpiece to one side of the dado. Lay out a line for the one side of the dado slot, and then measure the desired dado width and mark it. To mark the depth of the dado, draw a line across either edge. The dado depth is usually half the thickness of the workpiece. You can predetermine the depth of the cut by lowering the dado head to the top of the workpiece, barely touching it (Fig. 4-5A). Then, push the cuttinghead to the back of the travel arm (towards the column), and lower the arm by means of the elevating crank, counting revolutions until the desired depth is reached (Fig. 4-5B). *The tendency of the dado head to feed itself is even greater than for a single blade; there-*

fore, more control may be necessary to restrain this action.

Cutting Angle Dadoes. Miter angle dado cutting has many uses in cabinetmaking, construction work, and general woodworking. Among the other applications, the angle dado is used for recessing treads in stepladders, for joining the sill to the upright members of a window frame, to recess the narrow strips in shutters and louvers, and for dadoing stairway stringers. This cut is made in the same manner as the cross dado, except that the radial arm is moved right or left to the desired degree of angle as indicated on the miter scale (Fig. 4-6). Raise or lower the arm the desired depth of cut by means of the elevating

Fig. 4-6: Cutting an angle dado.

Fig. 4-7: Straight parallel dadoes.

crank. To make long cuts, simply move the table fence to the rear of the worktable.

Cutting Parallel Dadoes. These are a series of dado cuts exactly parallel to one another. With the radial saw, these cuts are easy to make because the material remains stationary, the cuttinghead doing the moving. As a result, any two cuts made with the machine in the same position (whether crosscut or any degree of miter) are always exactly parallel to one another. Mark the table fence and make successive cuts the exact distance apart (Fig. 4-7). Align the last finished dado with the fence mark for each succeeding dado to be cut.

When a number of pieces are to be identically dadoed, arrange the pieces as shown in Fig. 4-8. Once the first cut is made, lock all pieces squarely together with a scrap board of suitable length and thickness. Then use the series dado technique just described, for additional "ganged," spaced dado cutting.

Cutting Stopped and Blind Dadoes. A stopped dado is cut only partly across the workpiece. With the workpiece against the fence, mark off where you wish the dado to stop on the surface of the stock. With the dado head in the crosscut position and the arm set at the proper height, pull the carriage and yoke forward until the desired forward travel is determined. Then place a stop clamp on the machine as shown in Fig.

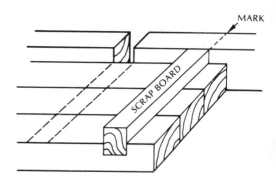

Fig. 4-8: Technique for cutting "ganged" spaced dadoes.

4-9A. Return the cuttinghead behind the fence, position the workpiece, and pull the cuttinghead forward until it hits the stop (Fig. 4-9B). Turn the saw OFF; when it has stopped, return the cuttinghead and remove the workpiece. Because the dado head is circular, the finished blind dado will diminish in depth as it nears the point at which it is stopped. The shallow surfacing end of the blind dado can be squared to uniform depth with a hammer and wood chisel. Stopped grooves can be cut in the rip position, using a stop block clamped to the table or table fence to ensure the proper distance for the stopped end.

Blind dadoes start and stop short of the edges of the workpiece; they are stopped on both edges. Both the start and finish

A

B

Fig. 4-9: (A) Using a stop clamp on the radial arm to set the length of a stopped dado; (B) cutting a stopped dado.

Fig. 4-10: It is necessary to mark the start and finish lines of a blind dado.

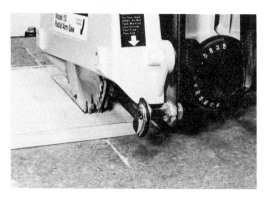

Fig. 4-11: Cutting a blind dado.

lines must be drawn preparatory to cutting (Fig. 4-10). The dado head must be aligned with the starting line, as above. Then turn the saw on, and with the carriage clamp knob locked, lower the revolving dado head into the clamped workpiece to start the cut. Use a clamp on the travel arm for the finish line of a blind dado, as for a stopped dado. Another even more efficient way of cutting blind dadoes, is to put two stop clamps on the arm, one for the starting line and one for the finish line of the dado. The revolving dado head is lowered into the workpiece and moved forward to the front stop clamp (Fig. 4-11). Turn off the saw and raise the arm until the dado head is clear. The workpiece can then be pulled from beneath the cutting tool.

Cutting Corner Dadoes. To make a corner-dado cut, place the workpiece at 45 degrees in a V-block and place the block against the table fence. Raise or lower the dado head until the proper depth is obtained. Pull the cuttinghead through the stock (Fig. 4-12) as in the standard crosscut procedure. The workpiece can project beyond the block, or the block may be partially cut away to permit the passage of the dado head. You can even use the V-block to form a dado in a cylinder.

CUTTING GROOVES

Grooving, or ploughing as it is sometimes called, is done in the same manner as straight ripping (Fig. 4-13). The table fence is used as a guide for grooving. To cut a groove, set the radial arm at 0 degrees on the miter scale (crosscut position); swivel the yoke 90 degrees from the crosscut position; move the carriage out on the arm to

Fig. 4-12: Cutting a corner dado, using a V-block to hold the workpiece.

Fig. 4-13: A typical straight grooving operation.

the desired setting and lock with the carriage clamp knob; and raise or lower the dado head to the desired depth for the groove. For a 1/4-inch deep groove, lower the column two turns of the elevating crank from a position where the dado head just touches the top surface of the stock. Adjust the blade guard so that the in-feed (front) part clears the workpiece, tighten the blade guard clamp knob, and then lower the anti-kickback fingers 1/8 inch below the surface of the board. Push the material against the table fence and past the dado head, against the rotation of the cutting tool in the same manner as when ripping.

If the cut is to be wider than the dado head, make several passes, overlapping them at least 1/16 inch. When making cuts more than twice the dado width, it is easiest to make the two outside cuts first; then to clean the center.

Cutting Bevel Grooves. This operation leaves a smooth, accurate V-groove in the workpiece. The cut has many applications, both functional and decorative, in cabinet-making and general woodworking. It also can be used to make V-block jigs. Bevel grooving is done with the radial arm and yoke positioned the same as for straight grooving. In this operation, however, the cuttinghead is tilted in the yoke to a 45-degree position. To tilt the cuttinghead, release the bevel clamp, tilt the cutting-

head in the yoke to the desired position, using the bevel angle scale, and then re-tighten the bevel clamp. The cuttinghead falls into the 45-degree angle positions automatically. (Other angles can be used and are located on the bevel angle scale and locked with the bevel clamp.) With the workpiece against the fence, move the cuttinghead out on the arm to the desired setting and lock the carriage clamp knob. Then raise or lower the arm to the desired depth for the V and push the workpiece past the dado head in the usual rip method.

While shallow V-grooves can be cut in one pass (Fig. 4-14A) deeper slots require two or more cuts (Fig. 4-14B). The cuts will be centered if a 45-degree bevel is employed for each. For uncentered V-grooves, make the two cuts at angles which will total 90 degrees (Fig. 4-14C). If you wish to make wider, flat-bottomed V-grooves, three or more cuts are required. Make the outside cuts first; then use a vertical blade setting to remove the middle portion and to produce the flat bottom (Fig. 4-14D).

Chamfering. Chamfering is just a V-groove that runs off the workpiece edge so that only the slope of the V is cut into the work. If this one slope is not wider than the dado-head, it can be done in one pass. Wider chamfers require additional cuts.

Fluting. This operation consists of making a series of V-grooves parallel to one another. Fluting is done with the cutting-

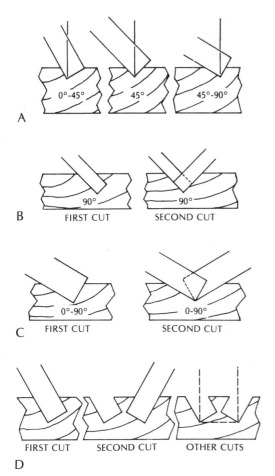

Fig. 4-15: A typical fluting operation.

Fig. 4-14: Cutting V-grooves: (A) in one pass; (B) with two cuts; (C) uncentered; (D) with a flat bottom.

head in the bevel-groove position. With many conventional-type woodworking machines, it is a real problem to get the grooves an equal distance apart and exactly parallel. This problem is eliminated with a radial saw because the rip scale allows you to position the cuttinghead exactly, and the table fence ensures that the cuts will be parallel. The elevating crank controls the depth of the cut, and the workpiece is pushed past the cutting tool as in all other grooving operations (Fig. 4-15). The finished cuts can be used to simulate pillars or columns in cupboards or fireplace mantels.

Cutting Gains and Blind Grooves. A gain is a groove that starts at one end and stops short of the opposite end. With the unit in the rip position, set the dado head to the desired depth of cut, and adjust the blade guard and anti-kickback fingers to their proper positions. Then feed the workpiece in the usual grooving method to the finish or stop line, or a stop block can be clamped to the fence or worktable (Fig. 4-16). Turn off the motor, and after the dado head has completely stopped, remove the workpiece.

Fig. 4-16: Using a stop block on the worktable to set the finish line of a gain.

A blind or center groove is a cut that starts inside of the workpiece and stops short of the end. This cut is achieved in the same way as for cutting a gain as described

59

above, except that the dado head is lowered to cut a groove as in blind dadoing. The difference is only the difference between ripping and crosscutting. If the stopped groove is to be cut in a long piece of stock, it may be necessary to clamp an auxiliary wood facing of suitable length to the regular table fence, and then clamp the stop blocks to this.

Panel Raising. Raised panels are used extensively in cabinet and door construction. This highly decorative and rich looking effect is very easy to accomplish on the radial saw with the dado head. Simply set up the saw for bevel rabbeting and "edge" the panel to a desired depth on four sides. The angle of the bevel will be the angle of pitch the resulting raised panel will have (Fig. 4-17). For best results, do the cross-grain cuts first, then do the cutting with the grain.

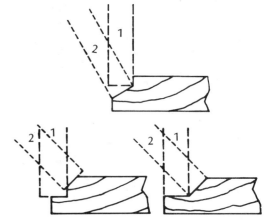

Fig. 4-18: Several different panel edge finishes, combining rabbet and chamfer cuts, with dado head positions and cutting sequences.

sired depth and pull it forward to the end of the cut; then raise the blade. Repeat this at the other end of the material. Then swing the arm into the rip position and cut grooves between the ends of the two dado cuts (Fig. 4-19). Proper stop clamps and stop blocks are necessary.

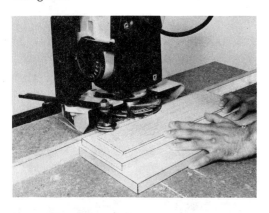

Fig. 4-17: Panel raising.

By combining rabbet and chamfer cuts, a wide variety of panel edge finishes can be obtained. Fig. 4-18 shows several interesting designs, and indicates the dado head positions and cutting sequences.

Panel Sinking. Another widely used decorative operation, panel sinking, is accomplished with a combination of cross dadoing and grooving. Lay out the desired design and locate the blade above the beginning of your first cross dado. Lower the rotating blade into the material to the de-

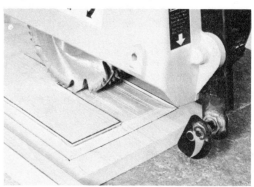

Fig. 4-19: Cutting dadoes and grooves for a panel sinking effect.

Lattice Cutting. This seemingly involved work is actually very simple to accomplish on a radial saw equipped with a dado head. The different patterns and designs of lattice and grillwork are limited only by your imagination. To make a lattice, simply make a number of parallel angle dado cuts halfway or slightly more than halfway through a board, then turn the work over

Fig. 4-20: A latticed panel is made by cutting parallel angle dadoes on both sides of the workpiece.

and make another series of matching cuts. The completed job will be a latticed panel ready for finishing (Fig. 4-20).

Horizontal Grooving. Generally, horizontal grooves are made on the side instead of the top or bottom surface of the workpiece. The arm is lowered so that the dado head is below the top surface of the stock. The finished cut is bound on two sides by the remaining stock, instead of on only one as with the rabbet cut (Fig. 4-21A). Using the dado head gives you an extrawide groove cut, eliminating some of the passes that are necessary when grooving with a saw blade. Blind horizontal grooving or blind mortising is similar to normal horizontal grooving except that the cut is not carried completely through the ends of the workpiece. In many cases, where the ends of the workpiece will be exposed, it is desirable not to show the side groove.

This operation requires the use of a special fence through which the dado head protrudes (Fig. 4-21B). The stop clamp is located on the radial arm to establish the forward travel of the cuttinghead (depth of cut of the groove). A stop block is clamped to the fence or table to locate the end of the cut. The workpiece is clamped to the fence at the beginning of the groove while the saw is turned on and fed to the stop clamp on the radial arm. Then the carriage clamp knob is locked, the workpiece is re-

A

B

C

Fig. 4-21: (A) A horizontal groove; (B) a special fence for cutting a blind horizontal groove or mortise; (C) cutting a blind horizontal groove, using a stop block to set the length of the groove.

leased from the fence clamp, and fed to the stop block, as in ripping (Fig. 4-21C). Then the saw is turned off and the workpiece removed. *Note: Use the molding head guard for all horizontal sawing operations; the guard was removed in the illustrations in this chapter for the sake of clarity only.*

RABBETING

Although rabbets can be cut by the repeat-pass method with a regular saw blade

61

(see page 49), the dado head makes the task a great deal easier. Rabbets can be cut with the dado head in the vertical or horizontal position. If they are made with the cutting tool in the vertical position (Fig. 4-22), the saw is set up in the normal crosscut position for an end rabbet and in the rip position for an edge rabbet (especially if the workpiece is too long to be easily cut in the crosscut position). Set the required depth and draw the dado head across the workpiece or push the workpiece through the dado head in the normal manner. To ensure accuracy, especially when rabbeting for joints, use a stop block setup that has been tested by making a test cut in scrap material.

Fig. 4-22: Cutting a rabbet with the dado head in a vertical position.

To cut a rabbet with the dado head in a horizontal position, elevate the arm until you have sufficient space beneath the cuttinghead to allow the motor shaft arbor to swing to a vertical position. Then release the bevel clamp and put the dado head in the horizontal sawing position. Then lower the arm to the desired depth for the cut and pass the workpiece past the dado head from the right side of the table using the table fence as a guide (Fig. 4-23). If thin stock is to be rabbeted, use the auxiliary table shown in Fig. 3-46 and set it in place of the standard table fence.

To lay out a rabbet joint, hold one edge of the stock to fit into the rabbet over the

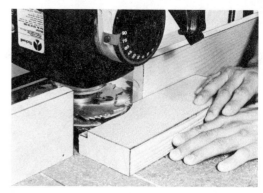

Fig. 4-23: Cutting a rabbet with the dado head in a horizontal position, using the table fence as a guide.

end or side of the stock that will be rabbeted, and mark the width of the rabbet. Then draw a line down the sides or end and measure one-half to two-thirds the thickness of the first piece as the depth of the rabbet.

Bevel Rabbeting. The bevel rabbet is made in a manner similar to the straight rabbet, except that the cuttinghead is placed at some angle less then 90 degrees (vertical position), depending upon the degree of the bevel desired (Fig. 4-24). This cut is widely used throughout construction, cabinetmaking, and general millwork operations. Blind or stopped rabbets can be cut by using one or two stop blocks clamped to the table or table fence to set the required rabbet lengths, or the rabbet dimensions can be marked. This operation is performed as described under horizontal grooving.

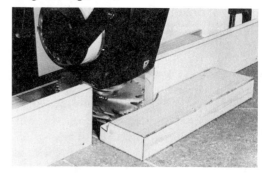

Fig. 4-24: A bevel rabbet.

Chapter 5

SPECIAL SAW OPERATIONS

As we already mentioned, there are only six basic saw cuts. However, by combining and varying these six cuts, it is possible to perform such special operations as taper ripping, chamfering, kerfing, cove cutting, or making saw-cut moldings, as well as to cut various rabbet, miter, lap, and assorted other joints. While these operations may seem more complicated than the basic cuts, they are easy and safe to do on a radial saw when the proper procedures are followed.

Kerfing. It is often necessary to bend wood. When the problem of curving wood surfaces arises, you have a choice of three methods: (1) bending the wood by steaming it (this calls for special equipment); (2) building the curve up by sawing thick segments of the circle on a saber saw (which means that a great deal of expensive wood would be wasted); or (3) cutting a series of saw kerfs to within 1/8 inch of the outside surface to make the material more flexible for bending. The latter—called kerfing—is the most practical method in the home shop (Fig. 5-1.).

The distance between these saw kerfs determines the flexibility of the stock and the radius to which it can be bent. To form a sharper curve, the saw kerfs should be as close together and as deep as possible. The first step necessary to determine the proper spacing, is to decide on the radius of the curve or circle to be formed (Fig. 5-2). After the radius has been determined, measure this same distance (the radius) from the end of the workpiece and make a saw kerf at this point. The kerf can be made in the crosscut position, with the blade set to 1/8 inch from the bottom of the stock. Next,

clamp the workpiece to the table top with a C-clamp. Raise the end of the workpiece until the saw kerf is closed, as shown in Fig. 5-3. The distance the workpiece is raised to close the kerf determines the distance needed between saw kerfs to form the proper curve.

A pencil mark should be made on the table fence, the exact distance away from the normal crosscut groove that will be needed between saw kerfs on the workpiece. As one saw kerf is cut, it will be lined up with the mark on the table fence and

Fig. 5-1: "Kerfing" is a practical home-shop method for bending wood.

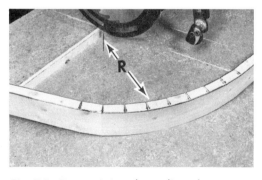

Fig. 5-2: Determining the radius of a curve to be formed when kerfing.

*NOTE: To clearly illustrate certain procedures described in this chapter, the blade guard and other safety devices have been removed. To safely operate the radial saw, the guards and other safety devices must always be utilized.

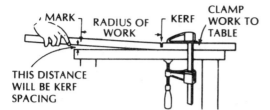

Fig. 5-3: Guide to figuring kerf spacing.

Fig. 5-4: Bending the kerfed workpiece.

Fig. 5-5: A type of dentil molding.

til molding," although this term has a broad application and is used to describe many other similar types of molding shapes.

The sawing setup for dentil molding includes the use of a simple auxiliary fence. A nail is driven into the fence to act as a guide

A

B

C

Fig. 5-6: (A) The distance from nail to blade determines the spacing of the saw cuts; (B) making repeated crosscuts for dentil molding; (C) ripping the molding into strips.

the next saw kerf will be cut, and so on, until the kerf cutting is completed.

When the kerfing is complete, the workpiece is slowly bent until it matches the required curve (Fig. 5-4). Wetting the wood with warm water will help the bending process, while a tie strip tacked in place will hold the shape until the curved piece is attached to an assembly. Even compound curves may be formed in this manner by kerfing both sides of the work. When kerfing 'is exposed, veneers may be glued in place to hide the cuts.

When bending wood for exterior work, the kerfs should be coated with glue before the bend is made. After making the bend, wood plastic and putty may be used to fill the crevices. When finished properly, only a close examination will show the method used to make the bend.

Sawcut Moldings. Several attractive moldings can be made with cuts similar to those used for kerfing. The zig-zag shape shown in Fig. 5-5 is commonly called "den-

pin for the work (or the regular table fence can be pencil-marked as in kerfing). The distance from nail to blade determines the spacing of the saw cuts (Fig. 5-6A). With the table fence in place, the saw is set at a suitable depth of cut and repeated crosscuts are made on both surface faces of the workpiece (Fig. 5-6B). The actual molding is then made by ripping off narrow strips (Fig. 5-6C). The material selected should be wide enough to allow the ripping operation to be performed easily and safely. A ripping operation on work as narrow and delicate as this demands care and accuracy. Use a push stick to feed the molding past the blade.

Molding should be cut with a hollow-ground or planer blade to assure clean cutting. After the dentil molding is cut, it can be used as an overlay, or the molding can be applied to a heavier backing piece of contrasting color (Fig. 5-7).

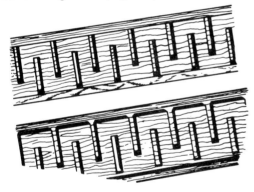

Fig. 5-7: Applying dentil molding to a heavier backing piece of contrasting color.

Other simple yet attractive moldings may be made with spaced saw cuts on the face of a piece of work (Fig. 5-8). Either draw the desired cut lines on the workpiece, or use the spacer pin to set the distance of the cuts in the same manner as when producing dentil moldings. When large grooves are needed, cut them with a dado. Once the design is completed, the molding can be ripped to the desired thickness.

Contour Cutting. Contour cutting, often

Fig. 5-8: Other attractive sawcut moldings.

called "radius" cutting, may be performed with a saw blade, but you will find it much easier and faster to do with a dado head. The concave cut resulting from this operation is quite frequently called for in furniture and cabinet production and is also used for making moldings of many kinds.

The saw is set up for contour cutting by tilting the dado head to a 15 degree bevel angle and locking it on the track arm over the center of the material to be cut. The dado head is then lowered until the cutter teeth are 1/8 inch below the top surface edge of the board. The board is then fed into the cutters along the fence as in ripping (Fig. 5-9). After each cut, lower the elevating crank handle one turn until the desired depth is cut.

Cove Cutting. Cove cutting produces a concave cut quite frequently called for in furniture and cabinet production and is used for making moldings of many kinds.

Fig. 5-9: Making a contour cut.

65

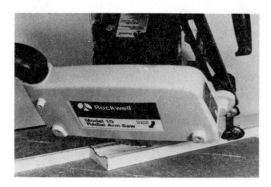

Fig. 5-10: The blade or dado head is set at any miter and bevel angle other than 90 degrees when cove cutting.

Cove cutting is quite similar to contour cutting. The difference is that the depth of cut may be increased without an equally proportionate *width* of cut resulting. The width of cut will, of course, increase with the depth but not to the extent predetermined by straight radius cutting. This may be accomplished by simply angling the blade into the cut. For instance, with the workpiece placed flat on the table against the table fence, set the blade at a 45-degree bevel position, and swivel the cuttinghead 45 degrees to the right. (Setting the blade at an angle other than 90 degrees in respect to the line at which the workpiece will be pushed into the blade is called *canting*.) Locate the cuttinghead so that the lowest point of the blade is on the center line of the workpiece and tighten the carriage clamp knob. Back the workpiece away from the saw and lower the blade so that it is 1/8 inch below the top surface of the stock. Turn on the saw and push the workpiece past the saw blade as when ripping (Fig. 5-10). Continue this procedure, lowering the blade one full turn (1/8 inch) at a time, until the desired depth of cut is obtained. The final cut should be a light one for a smooth finish.

The saw cut can be made in different angle positions for different effects. For instance, you could set the bevel at 45 degrees and swivel the cuttinghead 30 degrees, or set the bevel at 30 degrees and swivel the cuttinghead 45 degrees. Experiment with scrap wood until you get the effect you desire. It is possible to get some idea of what the cove will look like before starting the cut by using a parallel rule (Fig. 5-11). To use this rule properly, set the distance between the long arms to equal the width of the cove desired. Pivot the dado head or saw blade so that "front" and "back" teeth just touch the arm. The depth of the cove can be judged while it is being cut. But, when setting up the work for cutting, be certain the center line of the cove and the blade are the same.

Fig. 5-11: Using a parallel rule to determine a cove cut.

Another variation of contour cutting is making decorative cove-cut trim (Fig. 5-12). The trim can be made to any width or length desired. It has a series of equally spaced crosscut coves divided by dado-cut V-grooves. Make a mark on the table fence with guide lines on the work to obtain equal spacing. The trim can also be ripped into thin strips if desired.

Fig. 5-12: Making decorative cove-cut trim.

Circle Cutting. Circles of any size can be cut on the radial saw, using the technique shown in Fig. 5-13. A simple jig fixture is necessary. It consists of a 3/4-inch-thick board with an inverted fence nailed to one edge. The inverted fence is clamped in place of the regular table fence. This holds the jig. A nail, with the head cut off, is driven into the 3/4-inch board at the proper location. Then, the stock to be cut is pressed onto the nail and pivoted, as a series of crosscuts are made. Finish the circle by smoothing the circumference with a disk or drum sander.

Fig. 5-13: Cutting circles on the radial saw.

Fig. 5-14: Pattern sawing with the radial saw.

Pattern Sawing. The radial saw may be used to good advantage for pattern sawing production work comprised of straight lines. It is a very fast way of getting the work done and has a great advantage because it allows short pieces of waste stock to be worked to size quickly.

The general setup is shown in Fig. 5-14. An auxiliary table fence is clamped onto the regular table fence and the blade is set perfectly flush against its outer face. A pattern of the shape desired is then temporarily anchored to the material to be cut with finishing nails. After fastening it to the stock, the pattern is guided along the auxiliary table fence on each edge and the subsequent saw cuts produce a shape exactly similar to it.

A design can also be drawn directly on a workpiece, in which case no separate pattern is needed.

Squaring Small Stock. If scrap stock is within the crosscut capacity of the radial saw, it can be squared readily by four crosscuts. The first cut is made by visually lining up the cut on the scrap with the crosscut kerf on the table, being sure to hold the workpiece firmly. The resulting cut side is then placed flat against the table fence and the second cut is again lined up with the crosscut kerf. The remaining cuts are made in the same manner, placing the previous cut against the fence.

Cutting Compound Angles. Cutting compound angles on the radial saw is a fairly simple operation. Actually, a compound angle is a combination of a miter and a bevel cut. A compound angle made on the radial saw requires the cuttinghead to be tilted and the radial arm to be turned from 90 degrees (straight crosscutting position). Any frame or open structure with sloping sides requires a compound-angle cut. A chart on page 68 gives the saw set-

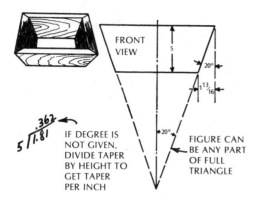

FRONT VIEW

5

20°

1 13/16

20°

FIGURE CAN BE ANY PART OF FULL TRIANGLE

.362
5 √1.81

IF DEGREE IS NOT GIVEN, DIVIDE TAPER BY HEIGHT TO GET TAPER PER INCH

Fig. 5-15: A four-sided miter box with sides tilted 20 degrees.

tings at 5-degree intervals for obtaining various compound angles. Cutting a peaked figure (with any number of sides) such as a doll- or bird-house roof or a fencepost top, and such house-construction jobs as cutting hip, hipjack, valley, and valley-jack rafters also require a compound-angle cut. Compound cuts are also required for making tables with splayed legs, if the outward tilt is more than 10 degrees.

A basic figure illustrating compound angles is a box (Fig. 5-15), which can have four, six, or eight sides, all equally tilted. The chart gives the saw settings at 5-degree

intervals, so the work should be planned to match. Joints for a four-sided figure can be either butted or mitered. Six- or eight-sided figures are always mitered because on such work a butt joint would be poor construction.

To joint two pieces of wood to form a 90-degree miter corner, you would set the radial arm at a 45-degree miter position. Strange at it may seem, when a compound-angle or shadow-box joint is made, the bevel that forms the miter must be cut at some angle, but it is never at 45 degrees. If for example, a shadow box is to be made, having the side slanting at 20 degrees as shown in Fig. 5-15, the angle at which the miter must be cut is 18.75 degrees and not 45 degrees, although when the pieces are assembled, the two 18.75-degree angles form a corner of 90 degrees.

Nevertheless, you don't have to know any geometry to make a cut for a shadow-box joint on the radial saw, if the chart shown on page 68 is used. The only thing you have to know is the slant at which you want to make the sides and whether you are making a box with four, six, or eight sides.

The use of the chart is quite simple and

TABLE OF COMPOUND ANGLES

Tilt of Work	Equivalent taper per inch	Four-Sided Butt		Four-Sided Miter		Six-Sided Miter		Eight-Sided Miter	
		Bevel Degrees	Miter Degrees	Bevel Degrees	Miter Degrees	Bevel Degrees	Miter Degrees	Bevel Degrees	Miter Degrees
5°	0.087	1/2	5	44 3/4	5	29 3/4	2 1/2	22 1/4	2
10°	0.176	1 1/2	9 3/4	44 1/4	9 3/4	29 1/2	5 1/2	22	4
15°	0.268	3 3/4	14 1/2	43 1/4	14 1/2	29	8 1/4	21 1/2	6
20°	0.364	6 1/4	18 3/4	41 3/4	18 3/4	28 1/4	11	21	8
25°	0.466	10	23	40	23	27 1/4	13 1/2	20 1/4	10
30°	0.577	14 1/2	26 1/2	37 3/4	26 1/2	26	16	19 1/2	11 3/4
35°	0.700	19 1/2	29 3/4	35 1/2	29 3/4	24 1/2	18 1/4	18 1/4	13 1/4
40°	0.839	24 1/2	32 3/4	32 1/2	32 3/4	22 3/4	20 1/4	17	15
45°	1.000	30	35 1/4	30	35 1/4	21	22 1/4	15 3/4	16 1/4
50°	1.19	36	37 1/2	27	37 1/2	19	23 3/4	14 1/2	17 1/2
55°	1.43	42	39 1/4	24	39 1/4	16 3/4	25 1/4	12 1/2	18 3/4
60°	1.73	48	41	21	41	14 1/2	26 1/2	11	19 3/4

can best be explained by an example. If a four-sided shadow-box frame such as is shown in Fig. 5-15 is to be made, with the sides slanting at an angle of 20 degrees, the information is applied to the chart in the following manner.

Because the box has four sides, and the joints are mitered, you only have to look for the settings under the 4-sided miter heading and across from a 20 degree tilt of work. You will find that you must tilt the cuttinghead in the yoke 41.75 degrees, and turn the radial arm 18.75 degrees on the

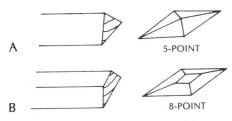

A

5-POINT

B

8-POINT

Fig. 5-16: (A) To make a 5-pointed diamond, the cross section of the stock must be an isosceles triangle; (B) a "triangle" with a flat top will make an 8-pointed diamond.

miter scale.

After the radial arm is set at the 18.75-degree miter position and the saw tilted to 41.75 degrees in the bevel position, place the workpiece against the table fence and pull the blade through it. Duplicate this cut (both right and left miter) for each end, positioning the workpiece as needed.

The settings for six- or eight-sided miters are found by making use of the appropri-

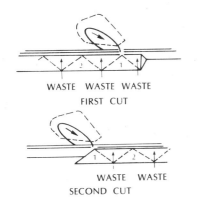

WASTE WASTE WASTE
FIRST CUT

WASTE   WASTE
SECOND CUT

Fig. 5-17: Cutting decorative diamond shapes.

ate column in the same way as for four-sided miters.

Chair and table legs are sometimes splayed outward. This construction calls for a compound cut at the top and bottom. If work of this type is done at less than a 10-degree tilt, a direct setting to the work tilt gives a satisfactory joint for these small angles. For a 10-degree tilt, the cutting-head is set at the 10-degree bevel position and the arm swung to the 10-degree miter position; for a 5-degree tilt as seen from the end, the bevel is tilted for one of the angles and the radial arm is swung for the other in the usual manner.

Decorative Diamonds. Diamond shapes involve another type of compound angle cutting and when properly cut, they can be assembled into decorative "stars," or

Fig. 5-18: Decorative pyramids can be made by cutting equally spaced V-grooves across the width and length of a workpiece.

be used singly to decorate workpieces. To make a 5-pointed diamond, a cross section of the stock must form an isosceles triangle (two sides equal—Fig. 5-16A). Any bevel angle can be used for the sides, but if a 60 degree angle is used, the cross section will be an equilateral triangle (all three sides equal). If the stock cross section forms a truncated triangle (one with a flat top), an 8-pointed diamond can be made (Fig. 5-16B).

To produce the diamonds themselves, two compound angle crosscuts are required. Tilt the cuttinghead to a 45 degree bevel angle, and set the radial arm for a 45 degree right-hand miter crosscut. Lay the triangular scrap against the table fence and cut off its right end. Then, turn the scrap around 180 degrees, using the same base of the triangle, and cut the first diamond from the left end of the scrap piece. Turn the workpiece 180 degrees again and cut the second diamond off of the right end of the stock (Fig. 5-17). Continue this procedure until the scrap becomes too short to hold safely against the table fence or the required number of pieces are made.

Decorative Pyramids. To achieve a faceted effect, flat-topped or peaked pyramids can be made by making equally spaced V-grooves both across the width and length of a workpiece (Fig. 5-18). Pyramids with square bases can be made by bevel crosscutting in both directions. Adding a miter angle by turning the radial arm will produce pyramids with a diamond-shaped base. Numerous variations can be made by altering the bevel or miter angles or the spacing of the grooves. For best results, do the crossgrain cuts first.

Taper Ripping. Taper cuts, needed for many projects, call for a jig with one straight side for riding the table fence and an angled side to gauge the taper. As illustrated in Fig. 5-19, various styles of tapered legs can be cut for furniture projects. Straight tapers, styles A, B, C, D, and E, are all cut with the radial saw. The various shapes are

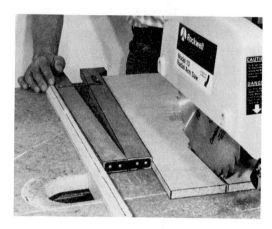

Fig. 5-20: The tapering jig in use.

Fig. 5-21: Using a template to make a taper cut.

often ornately carved, fluted, or inlaid. A planer combination blade is the preferable one to use for this work because it cuts more smoothly. Before using any jig, all edges to be tapered should be squared if uniform sides are desired.

When hinging the ends of the tapering jig, keep the two pieces clamped together. The crosspiece or brace which secures the setting can be made of hardwood. When the jig is complete, mark a line across both pieces, 12 inches in from the hinged end. Set the jig by measuring between these two marks to determine the taper per foot. The formula used for a so-called two-sided taper (actually, all four sides are tapered) is:

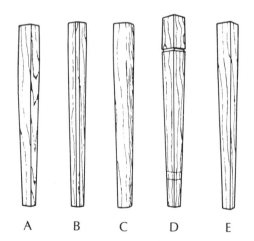

A   B   C   D   E

Fig. 5-19: Various examples of taper ripping.

$$\text{Taper per foot} = \frac{W \text{ (top width)} - W \text{ (bottom width)}}{L \text{ (length of taper)}} \times 6$$

For example, if you are making a coffee-table leg 18 inches long, 5 inches wide at the top, and 3 1/2 inches wide at the bottom, you would require a 1/2-inch taper per foot.

$$\text{Taper per foot} = \frac{5 - 3.5}{18} \times \frac{6}{1} = \frac{1.5}{3} = 0.5 \text{ or } 1/2 \text{ inch}$$

By opening the jig 1/2 inch at the 1-foot mark, you have the proper setting.

For a so-called one-sided taper (two sides are tapered), use the following formula:

$$\text{Taper per foot} = \frac{W \text{ (top width)} - W \text{ (bottom width)}}{L \text{ (length of taper)}} \times 12$$

Using these dimensions, you would find the one-sided taper as follows:

$$\text{Taper per foot} = \frac{5 - 3.5}{18} \times \frac{12}{1} = \frac{3}{3} = 1 \text{ inch}$$

To use the jig, place the flat side against the table fence and place the stock to be tapered in the stop at the end of the jig. With the saw in the rip position, push the jig past the blade as if it were a normal ripping operation (Fig. 5-20). Continue the ripping operation on all four sides in the same manner.

When the project calls for a two-sided taper, double the jig setting for the second pass. Be sure that the first tapered side of the work is placed against the jig when making the second pass.

Square legs with a taper on each face are made by setting the location of the saw blade to equal the combined width of the jig and the work. Make one pass; then, make the second pass on the adjacent face. Open the jig to twice the original setting and adjust the blade so that the wide end of the workpiece just touches it. Make the third pass on the next adjacent face, and then make the fourth and final pass.

A step jig or template is good for produc-

Fig. 5-22: Using the front edge of the worktable as a second "table fence" for taper ripping long or wide stock.

tion work because it eliminates having to change the setting for different tapers. The steps gauge the taper, with the dimensions cut for the various tapers needed. One corner of the workpiece is placed in the correct step while the other end rides against the arm of the jig. The workpiece is placed in the first notch of the jig, and the combined jig and workpiece are fed into the blade with the saw in a rip position (Fig. 5-21). An adjacent side of the work is cut in the same manner. The two remaining sides are cut with the work in the second notch.

Tapering with a radial saw can also be done without the use of a specialized jig. This includes taper ripping long stock which cannot be handled in a jig. By simply clamping a piece of narrow stock or a straight edge to the lower edge of the material to be ripped, the front of the worktable top becomes a second "table fence" (Fig. 5-22). You can taper rip to any predetermined angle with this method. Just decide the degree of taper desired; then, clamp on the lower guide board accordingly.

The best blade to use for taper ripping is a planer blade, because it cuts more smoothly. However, if another blade is used, the taper cuts can be smoothed by making a light jointer cut on each of the four surfaces. Be sure to use the proper direction of feed: in rip, from right to left; out-rip, from left to right. When taper ripping, the blade guard and anti-kickback fingers are adjusted in the same manner as for straight ripping.

Occasionally, it is desirable to joint a tapered workpiece to a mitered one. A good example of this is when it is necessary to fasten a taper leg to a table skirt board. When the taper angle is known, the radial arm can be set at this angle and the cut made. But if unknown, the angle of the miter cut can be determined, using the following formula with reference to Fig. 5-23:

$$X = \frac{W - W_1}{2}$$

Line A is at 90 degrees to the leg top starting at W and Line B is parallel to the line starting at W 1. Use the distance X to draw the cut-line on the workpiece that requires the crosscut. It is common practice to make a trial cut on a scrap piece of the same dimensions first, to insure a proper fit.

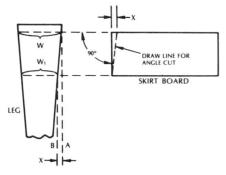

Fig. 5-23: Method of mating a crosscut miter to a taper.

Wedge Cutting. Any number of similarly shaped wedges or glue blocks can be cut by using a jig similar to the one shown in Fig. 5-24A. Cut the shape of the wedge or glue block into the edge of 1-inch template stock.

Set the cuttinghead in the in-rip position and adjust the blade so that it just passes the wedge cutting jig when it is against the table fence. Back off the jig and fit the

A

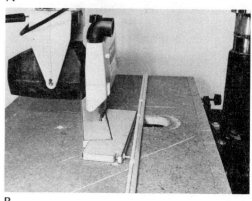

B

Fig. 5-24: (A) A jig for cutting similarly shaped wedges or glue blocks; (B) an adjustable jig for cutting wedges of different sizes.

Fig. 5-25: Cutting a tenon with a saw blade.

workpiece into the notch. Then move the workpiece and jig past the blade in the normal ripping manner. When cutting a series of wedges, reverse the stock from end to end for each new wedge.

Fig. 5-26: Cutting a tenon with two passes of a dado head.

Fig. 5-27: Using a dado head with a spacer collar to cut a tenon in one pass, using an auxiliary fence and table (molding head guard not shown).

Short wedges can also be cut in the normal cutoff manner with the arm in the proper miter position.

While a standard wedge cutting jig can be made easily for individual wedges, making an adjustable jig (Fig. 5-24B) makes more sense. A bolt, which can be seen at the front of the jig, is turned in or out, as required, to set the taper. The bolt head rides against the table fence. For occasional work of this kind it is more practical to make up a jig from solid lumber. This can be visualized by imagining the wedge formed by the bolt to be solid wood contacting the table fence. Never attempt to cut wedges freehand; always use some type of jig.

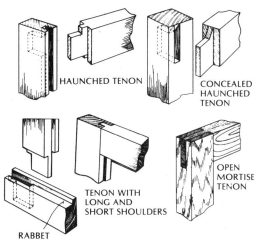

Fig. 5-28: The more common variations of the simple mortise and tenon joint.

WOOD JOINTS

The radial saw is an excellent power tool for fashioning wood joints. Some popular wood joints are described here.

Mortise and Tenon Joints. Since each face of a tenon is simply a deep rabbet, this portion of the joint can be done with a regular saw blade. The first two cuts are made on the top at the same tool setting; then similarly, the two side cuts are made at one setting (Fig. 5-25).

Tenons can also be cut with a dado head. Normally, inside chippers are used with the outside blades when making a tenon so that one side of the average stub is formed in one pass, the work turned over, and the stub completed in the next pass (Fig. 5-26). Normal crosscutting procedure is followed in the setup of the saw. When cutting extra-long tenons, begin with the inside cut and work toward the end of the stub in successive overlapping cuts.

Tenons may also be cut using a spacer collar between the dado head elements as shown in Fig. 5-27. A spacer collar equal to the desired width of the tenon is placed between the two blades normally used on the outside of the dado head. The chippers are placed on the outside, in this case, to remove the excess outside stock. The saw

A

B

Fig. 5-29: Using a dado head to make: (A) the tongue, and (B) the groove, for a tongue and groove joint.

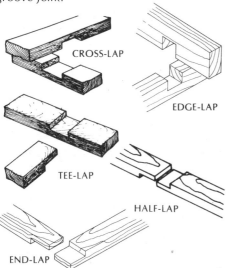
CROSS-LAP

EDGE-LAP

TEE-LAP

HALF-LAP

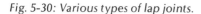
END-LAP

Fig. 5-30: Various types of lap joints.

A

B

Fig. 5-31: (A) On a cross-lap joint, the depth of the dadoes should be one-half the thickness of the stock; (B) cutting the end piece for a tee-lap joint.

is then set for horizontal crosscutting. An auxiliary fence and table, as shown in Fig. 5-27, is used to replace the table fence and to raise the workpiece to allow clearance for the arbor. The molding head guard should be used.

The stock is located against the auxiliary table fence and the cuttinghead is moved through the workpiece, completing the tenon easily and accurately in one pass.

Mortise and tenon joints are used more than any other type of joint in cabinetry work. There are a great many variations of the basic type to allow for the requirements of a specific job. A few of these are shown in Fig. 5-28. The mating mortise is cut with a mortising chisel in a drill press or with a router. A routed or bored mortise can be squared with a chisel, or the tenon can be sanded to fit the end radii.

Tongue and Groove Joints. The tongue and groove joint is made in the same manner as the mortise and tenon joint. Actually the tongue and groove is but a lengthwise variation of the mortise and tenon.

Use the auxiliary fence set up as described previously for the mortise and tenon joint, and adjust the dado head accordingly for the width of cut desired for the tongue (Fig. 5-29A) and for the width of the groove (Fig. 5-29B). Make the groove 1/32 inch wider than the tongue thickness, and 1/32 to 1/16 inch deeper; this makes for an easy fit. It is advisable to check the results of your original settings on a piece of scrap material of the same length as your proposed joint before proceeding on project material. Check to be sure the joint provides a smooth, flat surface on both sides of the stock.

Lap Joints. Lap joints take a great many

Fig. 5-32: The three-way lap joint.

forms (Fig. 5-30). They are best cut with a dado head. To lay out a *cross-lap joint*, mark a line across the surface of the one workpiece to indicate one side of the dado. Place the second piece over it and mark the width. Invert the pieces and mark the width on the second workpiece. Draw lines along the edges of both pieces and mark the depth of the dado, which should be one-half the thickness of the piece (Fig. 5-31A). The *edge-lap joint* is identical except that the workpieces cross on edge. The *middle-* or *tee-lap joint* is made with one piece exactly like the cross-lap joint

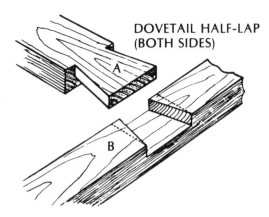

Fig. 5-33: The parts for a full-dovetail half-lap joint.

and the second piece cut on the end (Fig. 5-31B). The *end-lap joint*, which is used in frame construction, is made by laying out and cutting both pieces as shown. The *half-lap joint* is cut in the same way except that the pieces are joined end to end. The *end-lap* and *half-lap joints* are actually two tenons with the stock removed from only one side. With the cuttinghead in the vertical position, lay the workpieces, side by side, against the guide fence on the auxiliary table. Raise or lower the radial arm until the dado head is in the middle of the stock, and then pull the cutter through as in the

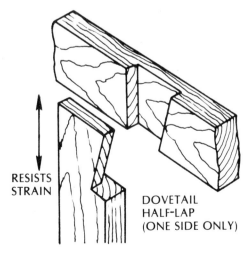

Fig. 5-34: The half-dovetail half-lap joint.

75

ordinary crosscutting procedure.

The *three-way lap joint* (Fig. 5-32) is accomplished by making all three cuts with the miter scale set at 30 degrees. It is used for jointing three pieces of wood while retaining a single thickness.

The *full-dovetail half-lap and the half-dovetail half-lap* joints are fancier versions of the tee-lap and cross-lap that are often seen in old cabinetwork. In both of these joints the dovetail is half-lapped into a rail, crosspiece, or upright, and the two pieces are joined at right angles. The main difference between the two is that the half-dovetail half-lap is not as difficult to make.

Piece B in Fig. 5-33 is cut first. Where the work permits, it is best to make the angle of the dovetail equal to half the thickness of the work, since this eliminates one setting of the saw. For example, if 3/4-inch stock is being worked, the dovetail should measure 3/8 inch. The miter angle setting for piece B is obtained by holding the work against the table fence of the auxiliary table and rotating the radial arm until a measurement taken from the outside edge of the dado head on the wider side of the dovetail to the line marking the outside edge of the dado head in a straight crosscutting position measures 3/8 inch. The dado head should be in a vertical position and set to cut half the thickness of the work. The other side is worked the same way, with the miter scale set to the same degree on the opposite side. Piece A is made by cutting the shoulder cuts on three sides. An end-lap tenon should be cut first with the dado head in a horizontal position. The sloping shoulders of the tenon are cut last, rotating the radial arm the same number of degrees as previously used for cutting Piece B.

The half-dovetail half-lap shown in Fig. 5-34 has only one side of the tongue and the dado cut at an angle.

Dado Joints. A dado joint is formed when one piece of wood is set into a groove or dado cut into another. While many different dado joints are used in cabinetwork

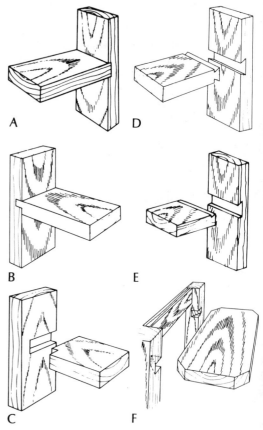

Fig. 5-35: Dado joints: (A) standard dado; (B) dado and rabbet; (C) stop dado; (D) full-dovetail dado; (E) half-dovetail dado; (F) corner dado.

and furniture making, the most commonly used ones are as follows:

The *standard* or *housed dado joint* is a groove cut in one piece of stock to the exact thickness of the second piece to be joined (Fig. 5-35A). All standard dadoes are best cut with a dado head, set to exact width. They can also be cut by making several passes with a single blade, then cleaning out the waste with a chisel. The dado can be cut at any angle to the edge.

The *dado and rabbet*, sometimes called a *dado box corner* or *dado and tenon* (Fig. 5-35B) is used when it is desirable to expose the cross grain at the side rather than at the end. If the dado, rabbet, and end lap are all of equal thickness, this gives a strong serviceable joint. The dado and rabbet can be used for drawer joints, but is also used extensively in shelf construction.

The *stopped* or *blind dado* (Fig. 5-35C) is a joint in which the cut is made partially across the first piece; then a corner is notched out of the second piece so the two pieces fit together. However, when this joint is cut with a dado head as described on page 56, a rounded surface forms at the end of the cut. This must either be cleaned out with a hand chisel or a notch must be cut to fit into the full depth of the dado.

The *full-dovetail dado* (Fig. 5-35D) is made by first cutting a dado to the narrowest width. Then replace the dado head with a single blade and adjust the cuttinghead to an angle of 15 degrees. Make the angle cut on both sides to clean out the mortise.

Fig. 5-37: Using the two outside dado blades to make a spline cut.

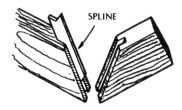

Fig. 5-36: A splined miter joint.

The tenon is cut in two steps with a single blade. First, cut the kerfs in the faces. Then adjust the cuttinghead to a 15-degree angle and make the two shoulder cuts. The *half-dovetail dado* (Fig. 5-35E) is cut the same way except that the angle cuts are made on only one side of the joint.

The *corner dado joint* (Fig. 5-35F) is cut across the edge of one piece, and the corner of the other piece is cut off to fit into the groove. Dowels are frequently employed to strengthen the joint.

Miter Joints. The miter joint is primarily for show. For example, it may be used for an uninterrupted wood grain around edges (side to top to side of a cabinet) or at corners (a picture frame). The joining ends or edges are usually cut at angles of 45 degrees, then glued, clamped, or otherwise fastened. Cuts slightly less then 45 degrees are often necessary when fitting new moldings on settled window casings,

but the differences are hardly noticeable once they are up and painted. In other words, there is a definite finished look to a mitered joint, whether it is left natural or painted.

The miter joint is worked flat or on edge (although an on-edge joint is also called a bevel joint). The setting of the cuttinghead in the yoke or on the radial arm, as required, is commonly a full 45 degrees and should be checked for accuracy on

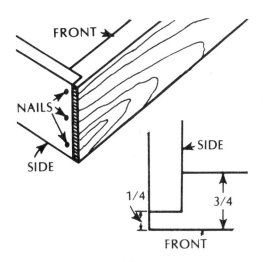

Fig. 5-38: A simple rabbet joint.

scrap stock before cutting the joint.

The Splined Miter Joint. The splined miter joint is simply a plain miter joint, cut with a saw blade, with a spline to give it added strength (Fig. 5-36). The spline, which can be hardwood, hardboard, or plywood, should always run the full length of the joint. The miter is cut with the radial arm swiveled to 45 degrees on the miter scale, using the table fence as a backstop for the workpiece.

Since a normal spline cut is about 1/4 inch wide in standard 3/4- or 1- inch stock, the job is frequently done by using the two outside blades of the dado head. In this case the cuttinghead is set for mitering to the required angle and the dado head blades then turned 90 degrees (parallel) to the table, in the horizontal position (Fig. 5-37). An auxiliary fence and raised table, as described for cutting a tenon, are required. The position of the material determines the depth of cut made; therefore, it is wise to work to a mark so that all your spline grooves will be of equal depth.

Stopped splined miters are cut in the same manner but the feed is stopped short of the outside edge of the workpiece. Use a stop clamp on the radial arm to control the length of cut.

Rabbet Joints. The rabbet joint is similar to a dado except that it has only two surfaces (a bottom and one side), and therefore, has to be made at the edge of your workpiece (unlike the rabbet, the dado occurs anywhere, except along an edge). This simple joint, extensively used in drawer construction, is pictured in Fig. 5-38. A fair standard with 3/4-inch front stock is to allow 1/4 inch for the lip. It can be seen that all of the work on the rabbet is on the front piece of the drawer. There is no work on the side. Methods of cutting rabbets are given in Chapters 3, 4, and 6.

CUTTING MATERIAL OTHER THAN WOOD

The versatility of the radial saw does not end with cutting wood. It can also be

Fig. 5-39: Make all crosscuts on plywood with the decorative surface face-up.

used with great success for cutting plastics, plywoods, hardboard, aluminum, ceramics, and many other building materials.

Wood product materials such as plywood and hardboard may be easily fashioned with little more difficulty than wood itself. The more exotic materials, however, call for some degree of special handling to get the best results, and to avoid harming the saw or saw blade.

Cutting Plywood. The best blades to use for cutting plywood are the special, fine-tooth plywood blades and the all-purpose, hard tooth, taper ground combination blades. The great number of teeth per inch, the thin rim, and absence of set (the outward angle of the teeth), allows the plywood blade to produce a very smooth, chip-free cut in plywoods of all thicknesses of up to 1 inch. The all-purpose, hard tooth combination has a set in the teeth and may not cut quite as smoothly, but it has the added advantage of cutting to a greater depth. Also, the hardened teeth will stay sharp longer. In addition to plywood, the all-purpose, hard tooth combination blade also produces excellent results when cutting limited quantities of hardboard and plastic.

With either blade installed on the radial saw, plywood may be shaped and fashioned in the same manner as regular wood. Make all cuts, other than for ripping, with the decorative surface face-up on the table, to avoid even the smallest amount of edge chipping (Fig. 5-39).

Cutting Plastic Laminates. This type of material is commonly used for sinks, table tops, and kitchen and bathroom splash boards. Although extremely hard and durable, plastic laminates are surprisingly easy to cut with a plywood blade. If you are going to cut larger quantities, however, it is best to use an all-purpose hard toothed or carbide-tipped blade because the standard plywood blade will become dull very quickly.

Always be sure to cut the material with the decorative edge face-up, except for ripping type cuts. This produces a smooth, clean edge on the surface. After cutting, round the corners of this edge slightly, for the sake of safety and to prevent chipping. Use a fine-tooth file or a plane to bevel the edge. Beveling will also correct any slight unevenness that may have occurred when cutting.

Cutting Wall Board. "Wall board" is the term used to classify such materials as asbestos, plasterboard, insulation board, and other materials that come in panel form. This material is easily cut and formed on the radial saw. The softer materials may even be cut with a knife and snapped off. The harder forms such as fiberboard can be cut quickly and very smoothly with a plywood or hollow ground blade. However, these materials are extremely abrasive and will quickly dull the blade.

Cutting Aluminum. Aluminum manufacturers produce a wide variety of aluminum shapes and extrusions that are becoming popular with the homeshop operator. There are a great number of aluminum forms that must be cut with special wheels or metal cutting blades, but most manufacturers are producing

Fig. 5-40: Score masonry materials 1/8 inch deep with the abrasive cutoff blade, then break them.

aluminum materials that may be worked with any standard saw blade.

For a fine, smooth cut in do-it-yourself aluminum, the plywood blade works very well, but the nonferrous-metal blade will probably be best. In many cases even the standard combination blade will produce good results. The choice of blade depends on the type, shape and thickness of material to be cut. For finer, faster cutting in thin walled tubing, use a fine toothed blade. For heavier gauge metal, a normal blade may be used.

Never force the blade or cut too rapidly. In aluminum, always advance the blade slowly and evenly, stopping the cut occasionally to allow the blade to cool down. A fast, heavy cut will cause the blade to heat up to such a point that bits of aluminum are actually welded to it. This will cause the blade to drag and cut roughly. It is also wise to clean the blade with a wire brush after each cut, while it is at rest, and to lubricate it with a light coating of paraffin or candle wax.

Thin walled round tubing is best cut by using a V-block, to hold the stock firmly in position. The V-block is clamped to the table fence and the workpiece is then clamped into the V-block at the correct length, and cut. Square or rectangular stock is cut flat on the worktable while held against the table fence.

The procedure for cutting this material is to take it easy and to allow the blade to remain cool as you cut, by letting it coast occasionally—never force the cut or feed too heavily. *When cutting material that can produce hot chips or sparks, remember that sawdust can be easily ignited. Always be sure that precautions are taken to remove flammable materials from the work area.*

Cut-off Blade Operation. Abrasive cut-off blades, also called abrasive wheels, can be used for cutting light metals, ceramics, porcelain, tile, brick, and similar materials. The reinforced blades commonly used are 8 inches in diameter by 3/32 inch thick, with a bonded abrasive (see page 11). Although these blades possess remarkable strength, they will chip or break if improperly handled. The feed should be steady and of sufficient pressure to prevent the blade from glazing. However, the work should not be forced too much, because this will shorten the life of the blade con-

siderably. Glazed ceramics and tile should always be cut with the glazed surface face up. Because cut-off blades are mounted on the primary motor shaft arbor as a saw blade, the blade guard should be used.

When cutting masonry materials, it is advisable to score them 1/8 inch deep (Fig. 5-40), then break the piece clean with a mason's hammer or a brick chisel. Score all four sides of thicker workpieces, so that the piece will break evenly all around.

A balanced blade or wheel with a clean edge is necessary for successful cutting. If the blade should get out of round, it will start to vibrate. This may result in a cut considerably wider than the thickness of the blade. Blade life is shortened, and precise cutting off is impossible. If the blade should get out of round or be chipped, it can be brought to a true edge with the use of a suitable abrasive stick.

When cutting material that can produce hot chips or sparks, remember that sawdust can be easily ignited. Always be sure that precautions are taken to remove flammable materials from the work area.

Chapter 6

MOLDING OPERATIONS

The molding cutterhead used with the radial saw is for straight shaping, matched shaping, tongue-and-groove cutting, planing, strip molding, sizing, ornamental and decorative shaping, functional shaping for glue jointing, door lips, or recessed drawers, and bevel and chamfer cutting. It is easy to perform these operations and to turn out this work quickly and accurately. In fact, the tilting motor-shaft arbor shaper of the radial saw may offer advantages over the conventional shaper. For instance, some standard makes of shapers are maneuverable in only two directions; the cutterhead can be raised and lowered, the table fence can be moved forward and backward. But unlike the radial saw shaper, on some standard shapers there is no provision for tilting the arbor or the cutterhead. This flexibility adds approximately 50 percent more shapes to each cutter. Also, you can shape in the center of wide stock, which is impossible with the limited spindle capacity of ordinary shapers.

THE MOLDING CUTTERHEAD AND ACCESSORIES

Nearly all common moldings can be cut on the radial saw with a molding cutterhead. There are several types of cutterheads available, but the common three-knife style is recommended for its strength and versatility (Fig. 6-1). There are many different cutting-knife shapes. The home-shop operator can start a cutting-knife collection with a few basic types, then add new ones as they are needed. There are also combination blades that permit different cuts, depending on which part of

Fig. 6-1: The common three-knife style of molding cutterhead.

the contour you use (Fig. 6-2).

As shown in Fig. 6-3, the special molding cutterhead guard totally encloses the cutting knives and the motor shaft arbor spindle. This guard is used for all molding operations with the cuttinghead in a vertical position (putting the molding cutterhead in a horizontal position). For any molding operations with the cuttinghead in a horizontal position (putting the molding cutterhead in a vertical position) the standard blade guard is used. The molding cutterhead guard is fitted on the cuttinghead exactly the same way as the standard blade guard. It has its own tightening screw to lock it on the cuttinghead collar. To allow the circular wall of the guard to be raised to a height permitting the user to check the precision of the cut, two screws, located on either side of the center screw, allow the protecting portion of the guard to be freely raised and lowered. When raised and locked into position by retight-

*NOTE: To clearly illustrate certain procedures described in this chapter, the blade guard and other safety devices have been removed. To safely operate the radial saw, the guards and other safety devices must always be utilized.

81

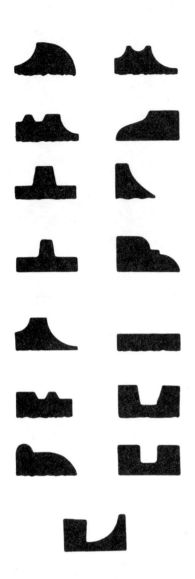

Fig. 6-2: Shapes of cutting knives used on the molding cutterhead.

Fig. 6-3: A typical molding cutterhead guard, used for all horizontal operations.

ening the two side screws, the molding cutterhead guard permits full access to the cutting knives. You can look and reach beneath the guard—always with the motor OFF—to position the knives accurately for the desired depth of cut. The easiest way to do this is to place the stock against the knives. After all adjustments have been made, the guard can be lowered to the top surface of the workpiece, and the molding,

jointing, or shaping operation can begin. *For the purpose of clarity, the guard has been left off in some of the photographs in this chapter. Always use a cutter guard or standard blade guard when performing molding and shaping operations on the radial saw.*

When using the molding cutterhead, it is necessary to make a special auxiliary, adjustable table fence (Fig. 6-4). The reasons for this are readily apparent. When stock is pushed along the table fence for a rip cut with a normal saw blade, the width of the workpiece does not change during the course of the cut. However, during some molding or shaping operations, stock will be removed from the entire edge of the workpiece. Therefore, if the standard table fence is used, the workpiece will not receive a straight cut (Fig. 6-5), because the outfeed side of the board may be narrower than the infeed side.

The auxiliary fence shown in Fig. 6-4 is actually comprised of two separate components, one on each side of the molding cutterhead. To install the auxiliary fence, place the standard table fence in the rearmost position, as you would to gain clearance for a left-hand miter cut. The back of the infeed half of the auxiliary fence is then butted against the standard fence;

82

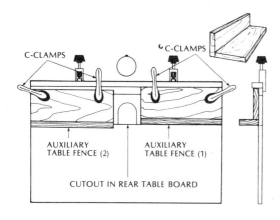

Fig. 6-4: A special auxiliary, adjustable fence for molding operations.

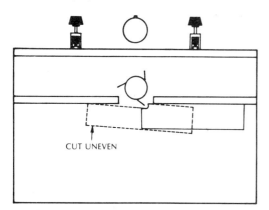

CUT UNEVEN

Fig. 6-5: Using a non-adjustable fence for shaping will result in uneven cuts.

the outfeed fence is adjusted to suit the type of cut being made. Both are independently clamped to the rear table boards. The fence should always be high enough to handle wide molding.

Figure 6-6 shows the action of the molding head, extending through the high auxiliary table fence and completing the decorative shape on the face of the stock. A "hold-in" feather board can be bolted to the wooden table top for a more accurate and efficient operation. Like the high table fence, this hold-in device can be made quickly and easily from lumber you will probably have on hand (Fig. 6-7). In addition to the board itself (slotted to allow for varying widths of stock), you

need only two C-clamps which will hold it firmly to the worktable top.

Also, because most molding operations are done with the cutterhead in a horizontal position, it is necessary to make an auxiliary table board with a cutout or a hole can be cut in the rear table board (Fig. 6-4), to allow the motor shaft arbor and the arbor nut to pass below the surface of the table. Finally, it is a good idea to glue or brad a piece of hardboard or similar material to the front table board, to ensure maximum clearance for cutting, as well as for a smooth surface to minimize friction.

Fig. 6-6: The molding operation.

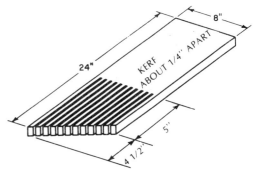

Fig. 6-7: A "hold-in" feather board for holding stock against the table fence.

THE MOLDING SET-UP AND BASIC OPERATIONS

On the typical radial saw, the molding cutterhead is placed on the primary motor shaft in the same manner as a regular saw blade. Place the arbor collars (3/8-inch collar first), the molding cutterhead, and the arbor nut on the motor shaft arbor, being sure the cutterhead is rotating in the right direction. Be certain that the knives are in place and tightened securely as directed by the manufacturer. Never leave knives locked in the cutterhead after using them. In fact, it is a good idea to clear gum and sawdust off of the knives and coat them with rust preventative, immediately after finishing a job. Store them, being sure that the cutting edges will be protected from nicks. The head itself should also be cleaned, especially the slots in which the knives sit.

For the basic set-up, position the radial arm at the 0 degree setting—the normal crosscut position—and tilt the cuttinghead in the yoke to a vertical position with the primary motor shaft arbor pointing down. This puts the molding cutterhead in a horizontal position. The elevating crank is used to lower the cutterhead to the desired cutting position. Sliding the carriage along the radial arm to the front or rear, positions the cuttinghead so that the projection of the knives in front of the special auxiliary fence equals the depth of cut (Fig. 6-8).

Remember, the molding cutterhead operates the same as the dado head, except that the slot it makes will have the shape of the cutters being used, instead of the flatness of a dado or groove. Like the dado head, the molding cutterhead should never be used for through-cutting operations.

Straight Molding. The great majority of molding work is performed on a straight surface. The operation is performed in much the same way as when using the dado head for grooving. In some cases you may want to use the top edge of the cutter knives to mold the bottom edge of the workpiece.

All cuts should be made on the side of the workpiece facing the fence. On the radial saw the shape being cut is not affected by variations in the width of the

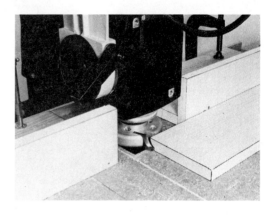

Fig. 6-8: Setting the depth of cut.

material as is the case when molding on the table saw.

When molding the perimeter of an entire surface such as a table top, cut the end grain shapes first, slowing down the feed when near the edge to prevent splintering. When the end grain surfaces are cut, make the with-the-grain cuts which will remove burrs and splinters on the corners (Fig. 6-9).

Attention should be given to cutting with the grain whenever possible as the resulting molding will then require little sanding to be entirely smooth.

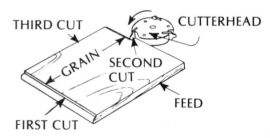

Fig. 6-9: When molding the perimeter of a workpiece, make the with-the-grain cuts last.

Strip Molding. A great deal of molding head work is in the form of cutting strip molding. Where only a few narrow strip moldings are needed, the operation is usually best carried out by molding the edges of wide boards and then ripping off the strips to the required width or thickness, as the case may be. However, when a quantity of the same molding is necessary, it is much quicker to use precut strips and a jig such as shown in Fig. 6-10. The jig must be securely clamped to the worktable. The precut strips, which should be at least 36 inches long, are fed into the jig by hand until the rear end starts to enter the jig. Then, the second precut strip or a properly sized scrap piece should be employed to push the first strip through the jig. The precut stock should be carefully selected for straightness of grain and lack of knots.

The jig is ideal for producing lightweight moldings such as the clover leaf strips used on screen doors and cabinet edges. It is also excellent for producing accurate moldings which require combination cuts, because the workpiece may be run through as many times as necessary to produce the required shape.

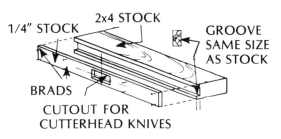

Fig. 6-10: A jig for making strip molding.

Jointing. In addition to molding, the cutterhead does a remarkable variety of jointing work. Glue, drawer, tongue-and-groove joints and a variety of others may be made with the cutterhead knives shown on page 82.

The *drawer-joint cutter* (Fig. 6-11A) is one of several one-purpose cutters. It is symmetrical and cuts both parts of the front-to-side joint. The front of the drawer is cut first; the depth of the cut is equal to the sidestock thickness. You can cut to within 1/8 inch of the front surface. The side of the drawer is cut with the work flat on the table. Test this on scrap stock to see how the joint fits.

The *symmetrical glue-joint cutter* is a one-purpose knife used only for making glue joints. The work must be exactly centered on the cutter, Fig. 6-11B. Properly centered, any two pieces will fit together when one of the pieces is reversed end to end. When the work has a definite face side, the reversal is done while cutting, molding one piece with the face side next to the table and the joining piece with the face side away from the table.

The *tongue and groove joint* is run with two cutters, one making the groove and the other the tongue. Both cutters are the same length so that, when the depth setting is made for one, the same setting is used for the other (Fig. 6-11C). All work is done in the same position, with the face

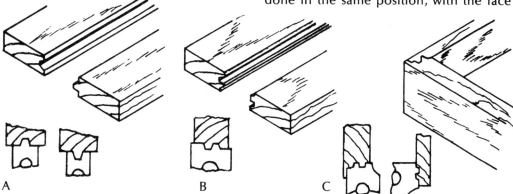

Fig. 6-11: Three common types of cutting knives for jointing: (A) drawer-joint cutter; (B) symmetrical glue-joint cutter; (C) tongue-and-groove joint cutters.

side to the fence. Tongue and groove cutters can also be used for drawer and corner joints.

Dowels. You may produce your own dowel rods with the molding cutterhead by using standard bead cutters (Fig. 6-12). Simply make light cuts on both sides of the stock until they meet at the center. The stock must be slightly thicker than the desired dowel. Remove the remaining thin edge with sandpaper and you have a well-made dowel.

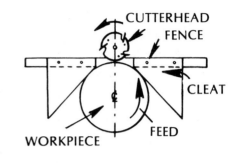

A

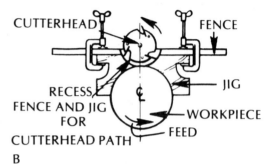

B

Fig. 6-13: (A) A jig for shaping circular material; (B) using the left-over scrap piece as a jig for cutting circles.

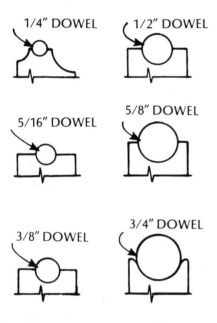

Fig. 6-12: Standard bead cutters can be used for cutting dowels.

Circular Molding. Circular material is best shaped with the use of a simple jig, such as shown in Fig. 6-13A. This set-up is made to hold the center line of the work against the jig. The workpiece is then rotated. A somewhat similar jig is shown in Fig. 6-13B. Here, the scrap piece, which is left after the circle has been sawed out, is clamped to the table fence to form a guide.

Both outside (Fig. 6-14A) and inside (Fig. 6-14B) curves can be molded, using a guide such as the one shown in Fig. 6-15, which causes full blade contact to be made at the center line of the cutterhead.

Chamfer Cutting and Panel Raising. It is possible to cut chamfers (Fig. 6-16A) and do panel raising (Fig. 6-16B) with a cutterhead equipped with straight-edge knives. These operations are accomplished by placing the cuttinghead in either the in- or out-rip position (the former is preferable) and setting it in a bevel position. Any degree of angle can be placed on the edge of the stock simply by changing the bevel angle of the cuttinghead. Place the workpiece against the fence, place the carriage at the proper location on the radial arm, and lower the column to the proper depth of cut. Feed the workpiece slowly past the knives in the same manner as when ripping. When panel raising, as in other cuts where the work is molded on all sides, the end cuts should be run first so that the final cuts with the grain will clean up the work. Actually, any molding

A

B

Fig. 6-14: Molding (A) outside, and (B) inside curves.

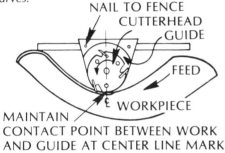

NAIL TO FENCE
CUTTERHEAD
GUIDE

FEED

WORKPIECE

MAINTAIN
CONTACT POINT BETWEEN WORK
AND GUIDE AT CENTER LINE MARK

Fig. 6-15: Guide for molding curved workpieces.

pattern desired can be cut on an angle or bevel.

Rabbeting. This operation can be done with a molding cutterhead and straight-edge knives (Fig. 6-17). This method is easier than the two-saw cut method, and is especially good for shallow cuts. For deep rabbet cuts, make several shallow cuts, lowering the cutter after each.

ORNAMENTAL MOLDING

A wide variety of ornamental moldings giving the appearance of hand-carved work can be made with molding cutters. Typical examples are shown in Fig. 6-18. The work is simply a repetition of any suit-

A

B

Fig. 6-16: Straight-edge knives can be used for: (A) chamfering; (B) panel raising.

able molding cut, the cuts being spaced by means of a guide pin and guide board. A guide board makes the best setup because many of the shapes cannot be spaced accurately with a pin set by itself.

The guide board is a separate saw cut strip made as illustrated in Fig. 6-19, and then fastened to the edge of the workpiece. The saw kerfs in the guide board are spaced to accommodate the particular cutter being used. The guide pin is a thin strip of wood set into a saw kerf on the auxiliary table fence. The pin may be located at any position because spacing is

Fig. 6-17: Using straight-edge knives for rabbeting.

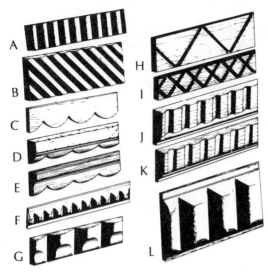

Fig. 6-18: Various ornamental moldings.

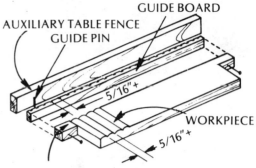

Fig. 6-19: Guide board for making ornamental molding.

Fig. 6-20: Making repetitive crosscuts to shape ornamental molding.

determined by the guide board and not by the workpiece.

The molding is produced by making repetitive crosscuts at the equally spaced intervals determined by the guide board (Fig. 6-20). When crosscutting with the molding cutterhead in a vertical position, use the standard saw blade guard, instead of the special molding cutterhead guard.

After the wide molding is complete, it can be ripped into suitable strips and further ornamented, if desired, by running molding cuts lengthwise on the strip in the ordinary manner. In Fig. 6-18, molding C is a thin slice of the bead shape. Shapes D, E, G, and L are thicker slices with lengthwise molding cuts added. Molding B is a small bead shape cut with the radial arm set at 45 degrees. Molding F is a small bead shape with the same cut returned along the edges to produce a rounded diamond similar to a sharp diamond produced with a

flute cutter. Molding H is worked with a flute cutter. Moldings J and K are cut with the cove-flute cutter, with a running molding added at the bottom. All molds shown are worked in the same general manner; first a wide strip is formed and then it is ripped into suitable narrow moldings.

Molding cutters must be sharp for this type of work because the work involves cross-grain cutting. Like other cuts of this nature, the end of the cut will tend to splinter out, if care is not taken when cutting.

Chapter 7

DRUM AND DISK SANDER OPERATIONS

Power sanding is the key to getting more productivity out of your shop. It removes the "bottleneck" that so often occurs between the final cuts and actually putting any project to use, because it saves hours of long and tedious handwork. It also provides a way in which true accuracy can be accomplished when finishing wood even to a very close tolerance. This is especially helpful when you are producing a number of pieces of cabinetry which must conform to the same basic design pattern.

Your radial saw can be quickly and easily adapted to perform a wide variety of power sanding operations. This is because of the great flexibility of the power unit, which can be turned and tilted in all directions. Of course, it is always better to have a tool designed specifically for doing a particular job, however, if you do not own a power sander, you can make use of the radial saw as outlined in this chapter to save time and work when finishing all your projects. *Proper ventilation in the work area is always necessary when performing any sanding operation.*

DRUM SANDING

Radial saw sanding drums are composed of a shaft directly attached to a circular base, or drum, which is made up of alternating layers of rubber and fiber. Two standard drum sizes are 3 x 3 inches and 1 3/4 x 2 inches. To use the drum, "load" it by placing on an abrasive sleeve of the desired material and grit. You then secure the sleeve by turning a spindle nut on the bottom which causes the drum surface to expand, pressing against the sleeve, and holding it in position.

There are a wide variety of abrasives and grit sizes available for sanding either wood or metal surfaces. The most popular of these, however, are the garnet and aluminum oxide sleeves. Garnet is a hard, rubylike natural abrasive, best suited for wood finishing. Aluminum oxide is a hard, tough material used for wood, plastic, and metal finishing. Either of these may be obtained in grit sizes for fine, medium, or coarse work, depending upon the requirements of the job. In general, coarser grits remove the most material in the shortest time. The fine grits produce a smoother finish.

Vertical Operation of the Drum Sander. Drum sanding on the radial saw can be done in the vertical, horizontal, and bevel positions of the cuttinghead. To sand vertically, remove the blade guard, arbor nut, cutting device, and arbor collars from the primary motor shaft arbor. Screw the sanding drum directly onto the right-hand auxiliary motor shaft arbor. Raise the radial arm and turn the cuttinghead in the yoke, putting the auxiliary end of the motor shaft arbor in a vertical position, directly above the worktable. Locate the cuttinghead on the arm and tighten the carriage clamp knob. The arm can then be lowered to the desired position.

Freehand Sanding. Sanding drums are very popular for freehand edge finishing. To set up the radial saw for this operation, it is a standard procedure to make use of an auxiliary table board, which allows the drum to be passed through it so that the entire edge of the stock being finished will come in contact with the abrasive. An

Fig. 7-1: A hole cut in the rear table board, to allow the sanding drum to be dropped below the surface of the table.

alternative is to cut a hole in the rear table board, as shown in Fig. 7-1. The material also may then be pressed against a surface of the drum which is firmer than its edge surface and therefore will give more accurate results.

When using a drum sander freehand, move the work past the drum from left to right. Also, keep it in constant motion to prevent overheating and scorching the wood. Wire-brushing the sleeve occasionally will prolong its useful life. Ordinarily, this is most effective if done while the machine is running.

Internal Sanding. Raise the radial arm so the workpiece can be placed under the

drum, and then lower it back into position (Fig. 7-2). Then proceed to move the work around as described for freehand sanding.

Pattern Sanding. The most troublesome feature of edge sanding with a drum sander is that if you hold the work a moment too long at any one spot, the drum immediately cuts into the work, causing a ridge. This can be avoided and perfect work done if a pattern is used as a guide (Fig. 7-3). Pattern sanding is very useful for precision production work.

The pattern is a full-size template of the desired shape, with the edges carefully finished. It is fitted with two or more anchor points. These can be wood screws, with the projecting end filed to a thin, flat point, as shown in Fig. 7-4. The work is fitted to the pattern, the anchor points holding it in place. Band, scroll, or saber sawing is then done, keeping about 1/16 inch outside the pattern. Figure 7-5 shows how the worktable is fitted with a hardwood guide ring or pin. When the pattern is pressed against the collar or pin, the drum cuts the work down to the same size as the pattern.

Miscellaneous Vertical Drum Sanding Operations. Circular work may be sanded easily with the drum sander by making use

Fig. 7-2: Internal drum sanding.

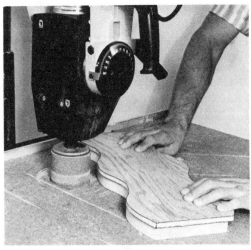

Fig. 7-3: Pattern sanding with the sanding drum.

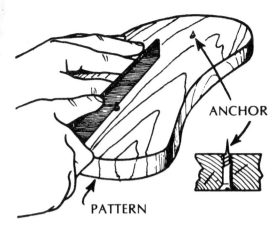

Fig. 7-4: Template used for pattern sanding.

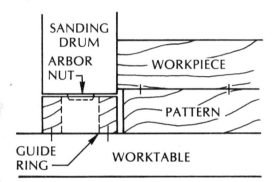

Fig. 7-5: A hardwood guide pin for pattern sanding.

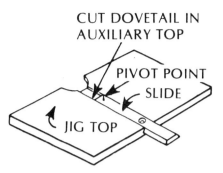

Fig. 7-6: A jig for drum sanding circular work.

A

B

Fig. 7-7: Straight sanding, using (A) an auxiliary table jig; (B) the table fence as a guide.

of a jig such as that shown in Fig. 7-6.

Straight sanding may also be accomplished much easier and with greater accuracy through the use of an auxiliary table jig slotted to accommodate a standard table saw miter gauge (Fig. 7-7A). Straight stock can also be sanded against a table fence (Fig. 7-7B). But in either case, be sure to keep the workpiece moving at a uniform rate, from left to right, past the drum. If the work is stopped at any point while in contact with the rotating drum, it may be scored or burned. Uneven feed can produce scoring at intervals along the length of the stock.

Bevel or Angular Sanding. With the radial arm in the crosscut position, turn the yoke to the out-rip position, and place the cuttinghead at the desired angle of bevel, as shown. Then feed the pre-cut stock against a fence and past the drum sander at a uniform speed (Fig. 7-8).

Horizontal Operation of the Drum Sander. In the horizontal position, the drum sander will do an effective job of surfacing narrow work when used as shown in

Fig. 7-8: Bevel sanding in the out-rip position.

Fig. 7-9. For this operation, use either the auxiliary or stationary table. With the cuttinghead raised to its full extent, set the auxiliary motor shaft in a horizontal position. Place the material tight against the table fence, and lower the radial arm until the abrasive hits the end of the stock. Withdraw the workpiece, turn on the motor, and feed the work against the rotation of the drum. If more smoothness is desired, keep lowering the arm a quarter turn at a time.

Wider boards may be handled in the same manner except that several passes will have to be taken with the sander at the same height. Remember, during any surface sanding operation do not attempt too deep a bite in one pass; two or more passes will result in a better job.

The radial saw can also be set up horizontally to freehand sand surfaces (Fig. 7-10) which cannot be laid level on the table. As with all drum sanding operations with the radial saw, the workpiece should be fed against the drum rotation.

Sanding Rabbets and Similar Cuts. Sanding the inside corners of rabbets and similar cuts can be easily executed with the drum sander as shown in Fig. 7-11. The rabbeted stock is set against the auxiliary table fence, and the drum is set to fit in

Fig. 7-10: Freehand sanding with the drum in a horizontal position.

Fig. 7-9: Surface sanding narrow work with the sanding drum, using the table fence as a guide.

Fig. 7-11: Sanding a rabbet with the sanding drum.

the corner. For operations like this, the sleeve should be mounted so that it projects about 1/32 inch beyond the bottom of the drum allowing the inside corner to be finished cleanly.

Concave Sanding. Fitting legs or rails to a round column or disk is much easier to accomplish when the work is sanded smooth with a drum sander. To be sure of maintaining the correct diameter of the cut, it is advisable to use a support such as that shown in Fig. 7-12.

DISK SANDING

The sanding disk can perform nearly every operation a sanding drum can, with the exception of smoothing small intricate cuts or internally curved surfaces. Its basic advantage is in the somewhat larger surface area it offers for general sanding applications.

To use the disk sander, position the saw in the normal cutoff position and replace the blade with the threaded disk. Most abrasive disks have pressure sensitive backs, making it unnecessary to use glue. Simply peel the backing from the disk, lay it on the metal plate, and smooth it out. It is easy to remove an old disk; just peel it off the metal plate. Best results will be achieved if the plate is thoroughly cleaned

before applying a new disk. The abrasive disks, like sanding sleeves, are available in various grits and grades, dependent upon the cutting action required.

Since most of the work you will handle will need to be elevated above the surface of the table so that the disk may turn freely without rubbing it, an auxiliary table jig, similar to the one shown in Fig. 7-13, should be constructed. It will facilitate the handling of not only freehand work, but can also be a great aid in performing accurate straight and circular sanding.

Use a smooth, light, and continuous feed when sanding, and avoid heavy pressure. Best results, especially on curved work, can be obtained by going over the work with two or three light cuts. Also, remember to always feed the work into the "down" side (right) of the disk. Working on the "up" side causes the material to lift away from the table.

Butt and Miter Sanding. A table saw miter gauge on the auxiliary table jig (Fig. 7-14) can be helpful for accurately sanding square or beveled edges.

The simple auxiliary table jig illustrated in Fig. 7-13 is also good for both butt and miter sanding. To butt sand, place the cuttinghead in the crosscut position and set the auxiliary table jig in place of the table

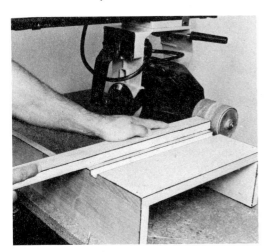

Fig. 7-12: Concave sanding.

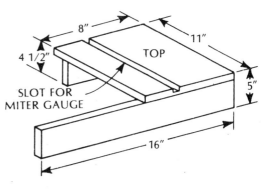

Fig. 7-13: An auxiliary table jig to raise stock off the worktable for disk sanding.

93

Fig. 7-14: Using a table saw miter gauge for disk sanding on the radial saw.

Fig. 7-15: Butt sanding with the sanding disk.

fence. With the workpiece tightly against the fence of the auxiliary table and making contact with the disk, pull the cuttinghead past the workpiece in the same manner as when crosscutting (Fig. 7-15). If you are doing fine butt sanding, swing the cuttinghead 1 to 3 degrees to the left, rotating and clamping the cuttinghead under the carriage, for the down rotation operation.

To miter sand, place the sanding disk in the crosscut position and locate the radial arm at the desired miter angle. Position the workpiece on the auxiliary table jig so it contacts the abrasive; then pull the sanding disk across the miter end of the board (Fig. 7-16). If finer sanding is

required, again swivel the cuttinghead 1 to 3 degrees to the left.

Bevel Sanding. With the radial arm in the crosscut position, place the cuttinghead at the desired angle of bevel and locate the auxiliary table in place of the table fence. Position the workpiece on the jig so it contacts the sander. Pull the disk across the beveled end of the board (Fig. 7-17). As in butt sanding, swinging the cuttinghead 1 to 3 degrees to the left will produce a finer job.

To sand compound angle work, swing the radial arm to the desired miter angle and place the blade at the proper bevel angle. Then, set the precut stock on the auxiliary table and pull the disk across the board.

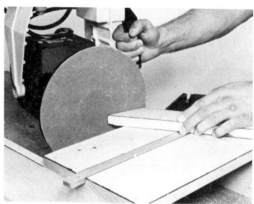

Fig. 7-16: Miter sanding with the sanding disk.

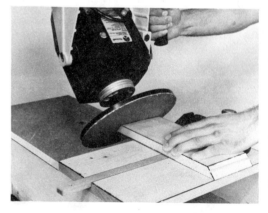

Fig. 7-17: Disk sanding the beveled end of a board.

Sanding Circles. Whenever possible, use a pivot when sanding circular work. A pivot point may easily be added to the disk sanding table shown in Fig. 7-13, or be made simply by driving a brad into a board clamped to the sanding table at the required distance from the sanding disk. For more accurate results or for production work, the pivot jig illustrated in Fig. 7-18 can be most useful.

When sanding a "perfect" circle, start with a square board; to find the exact center of the square, draw two diagonal lines from each corner. Then cut the square down to the approximate circumference of the circle on a band saw or saber saw. Place the cuttinghead in the crosscut position. Lower the radial arm to the proper height and lock it in place directly in front of the jig.

To use the jig (Fig. 7-18), first lock the sliding strip in place at the required distance from the face of the sanding disk. A pencil mark is then drawn on the jig table, the same distance from the pivot point as the pivot point is from the sanding disk.

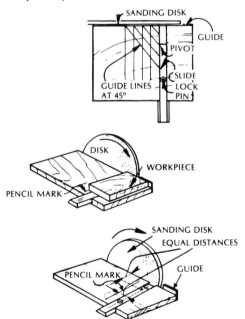

Fig. 7-18: A pivot jig for sanding circular work.

Place the workpiece against the guide and bring it into alignment with the pencil mark. Turn on the machine and slowly rotate the workpiece on the pivot pin (moving it closer to the disk from time to time) until it is perfectly round and uniformly smooth (Fig. 7-19).

Fig. 7-19: Using the pivot jig to sand a circular workpiece.

Rounding Corners. The sanding of corners is allied to circular work in that the edge being worked is part of a true circle. Most work of this nature can be done freehand, sweeping the corner of the work across the face of the sanding disk two or three times until the desired radius is obtained (Fig. 7-20).

Fig. 7-20: Rounding corners freehand with the sanding disk.

95

Pattern Sanding. To use the disk sander for pattern sanding, fasten a thin but rigid strip of metal on the sanding table as shown in Fig. 7-21. An undersized pattern is required. The amount of undersize is determined by the distance from the metal guide to the disk surface. Use the same type of pattern anchor point set up that is used for drum sanding (Fig. 7-4). In this case, however, hold the pattern in contact with the metal guide as it moves for a smooth uniform finish (Fig. 7-22).

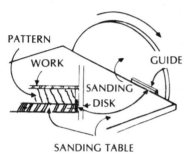

Fig. 7-21: *Setup for pattern sanding, using the sanding disk.*

Fig. 7-22: *Pattern sanding with the sanding disk.*

Surface Sanding. To position the machine for general surfacing, elevate the radial arm until the cuttinghead with the disk attached can be tilted to the vertical position. Then move the cuttinghead along the arm until the disk is directly above the path the material will follow along the table fence, and lock it into position with the carriage clamp knob. Place your stock on the table and lower the arm until the disk fits snugly against the top surface of the board. Then push the board from right to left along the table fence (Fig. 7-23). For extra fine sanding, raise the cuttinghead from the 90-degree bevel position 1 to 3 degrees (indicated as 89 to 87 on the bevel scale). In this position, the sanding will be done on the downside portion of the disk.

Sanding Plastics and Metals. Finishing plastics and metals with the disk sander (as well as the drum sander) is the same as similar operations on wood, with the exception that a different abrasive (usually aluminum oxide) should be used. Generally, the feed with these materials should be less and the pass made more slowly.

Fig. 7-23: *Surface sanding along the guide fence.*

Chapter 8

OTHER USES OF THE RADIAL SAW

Although radial saws are used primarily for various cutting, shaping, jointing, and sanding operations, many radial saws can be equipped for several other types of work. The typical radial saw can be easily adapted for assorted boring (drilling holes in wood), routing, buffing, and polishing operations. In fact, it is this wide versatility which makes the radial saw such a valuable addition to any home or production workshop.

As a boring tool, the radial saw even overcomes certain limitations of the conventional drill press. For example, you are not restricted by the length or width of the material you can bore because of the throat opening or the length of the downstroke of the drill press. The boring action of the radial saw is horizontal rather than vertical (Fig. 8-1). Therefore, workpieces several feet in length can be end-bored with precision and accuracy. The depth of the hole to be bored is limited only by the length of the bit itself, not by the stroke of the press.

BORING OPERATIONS

For various boring operations, a simple jig (Fig. 8-2A) is needed to raise the workpiece above the surface of the worktable top and to provide a higher table fence. Place a wedge between the jig and the column to add support when drilling (Fig. 8-2B).

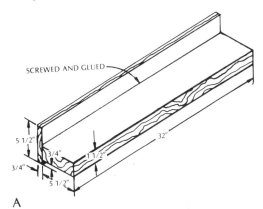

A

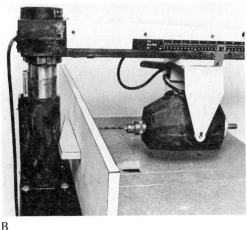

B

Fig. 8-2: (A) A simple auxiliary table jig for boring operations; (B) a wedge between the auxiliary table jig and the column to give added support.

Fig. 8-1: The boring action of the radial saw is horizontal.

Laying Out the Work. An accurate layout is a basic requirement for boring holes. The simplest method of marking the location of a hole is to draw lines which intersect at the center of the hole. For such work, a combination square is ideal, since it can be used to draw lines parallel with the edge of the workpiece and as an edge-marking gauge. Dividers are handy when it is necessary to transfer a measurement from one piece to another or to mark off a line in a number of equal spaces. If a pencil is used for marking, select a hard one (3H or harder) and keep it sharp so that the lines will be well defined.

Mounting the Bit. To mount the boring bit, remove the blade guard, the arbor nut, the cutting device, and the arbor collars from the primary motor shaft. The right hand auxiliary motor shaft arbor will accommodate a 1/2-inch capacity key chuck and uses common right hand rotation bits. Because of the motor speed, however, there is some limitation on the type of bit which can be used. Multi-spur bits, expansive bits, and drill bits more than 3/4 inch in diameter, require a slower speed than that developed by the radial saw. Although the radial saw offers certain advantages for boring operations, it must be remembered that this power tool is not primarily intended for boring. Some types of work done on a conventional drill press cannot be done as easily or as well on a radial saw.

Face Boring. Locate the center of the hole and mark it with a scratch awl. Insert the proper bit in the chuck; then tighten the chuck with the chuck key (Fig. 8-3). *Always remember to remove the chuck key before turning the radial saw on.* Bring the cuttinghead forward to the front of the arm and swing it in the carriage, so that the bit will face toward the column of the saw. Set the workpiece on edge on top of the boring jig against the table fence. Raise or lower the radial arm so that the bit touches the workpiece at the desired spot. Turn the saw on, and slowly push the carriage

Fig. 8-3: Tightening a geared chuck with a chuck key.

backward on the arm until the bit has entered the workpiece to the desired depth. Hold the workpiece firmly and apply even pressure to the carriage and cuttinghead. If the workpiece is hardwood or the hole is deep, back out the bit once or twice to remove the chips before finishing the hole.

For boring more than one hole of the same depth, place a stop clamp on the arm (Fig. 8-4) to limit the travel of the head.

If you plan to bore all the way through the stock, place a piece of scrap wood behind the hole location. Always bore through the hole and into the scrap wood. If no backup board is used, the wood will splinter as the bit goes through the workpiece.

Fig. 8-4: A stop clamp on the arm to set the depth of the hole when face boring.

End Boring. Place the workpiece flat on the boring jig (Fig. 8-5A) and against the table fence. Place the cuttinghead in the standard crosscut position, move the carriage on the radial arm so that the bit touches the workpiece at the desired spot, and lock with the carriage clamp knob. Then push the workpiece into the bit until the hole is of the desired depth (Fig. 8-5B). On deep holes, back off from the bit once or twice to remove the chips.

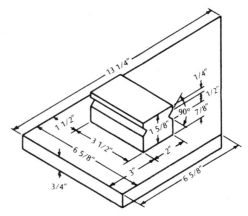

A

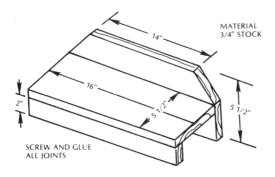

MATERIAL 3/4" STOCK

SCREW AND GLUE ALL JOINTS

A

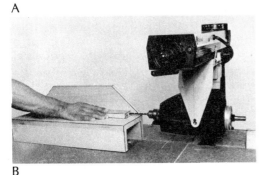

B

Fig. 8-5: (A) A jig for end boring; (B) the end boring operation.

Miter Boring. Miter joints are often strengthened with dowels; the dowel holes can be drilled with the radial saw. Using the same jig, and with the cuttinghead placed exactly as for end boring, push the workpiece into the bit at any desired angle. Use a push board (Fig. 8-6A) with a mitered end to direct the workpiece into the bit at the proper angle (Fig. 8-6B). Note that since the bit remains stationary it is possible to drill holes in the same position on the ends of more than one piece of stock.

B

Fig. 8-6: (A) A push board for miter boring; (B) the miter boring operation.

When moving for a second hole, the in-rip scale on the right side of the radial arm makes the precise placing of the bit an easy job.

Parallel Boring. This is making a series of holes in the manner described for face boring. Because the workpiece remains positioned at exactly the same level on the boring jig, and the bit enters at exactly the same height (riding on the tracks inside the radial arm), the holes will be parallel to one another (Fig. 8-7A). Parallel boring can be done in the vertical position, too. Bore the holes evenly by lowering or raising the radial arm with the elevating crank the same number of turns for each hole (Fig. 8-7B).

When boring equal-depth holes at the end of a board, using a stop block simplifies the work, as shown in Fig. 8-7C.

A

B

A

B

Fig. 8-8: (A) Boring round stock against the auxiliary table fence; (B) boring holes in a circular piece, nailed and pivoted on the auxiliary table fence.

C

Fig. 8-7: (A) Horizontal parallel boring; (B) vertical parallel boring; (C) using a stop block to ensure equal-depth holes.

Boring in Round Stock. Round work can be pushed tight against the table fence and jig table or V-block and held as shown in Fig. 8-8A. The hole is then bored as described for face boring. To bore holes around a circle, either on a disk or some other shape, pivot the workpiece on the center of the circle, using a bolt through the piece or a nail filed to a point and driven into an auxiliary table (Fig. 8-8B).

Boring in Circular Stock. Circular stock should be securely clamped to a suitable work surface before it is edge or surface bored. As with round stock, a secure grip is necessary to get perfectly aligned holes in circular stock, and to insure against the workpiece slipping or rolling.

Angular Boring. The workpiece is positioned on the jig exactly as for face boring. The radial arm, however, is moved either to the right or left so that the bit will enter the workpiece at any desired angle when pushed back on the arm (Fig. 8-9). The miter scale at the top of the column allows you to determine the angle at which the bit will enter.

Boring Mortises. Very good mortises with round ends can be bored on the radial saw in the same manner as edge boring. First determine the depth of the mortise and set a stop clamp on the radial arm. Bore the first hole at the point where the left end of the mortise is to be cut. Bore the

Fig. 8-9: Angular boring.

holes fairly close together; then bore other holes between, as shown by the dotted lines in Fig. 8-10. The tenon for a round-end mortise can be cut as described on page 73 and rounded off on the disk sander.

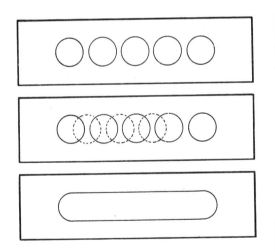

Fig. 8-10: Boring a series of holes to make a mortise.

ROUTING

The radial arm saw can be quickly converted into a router, by removing the safety guard, the arbor nut, the cutting device, and the arbor collars from the primary motor shaft arbor, and placing the router bit adaptor on the auxiliary motor shaft arbor. The router bit adaptor holds stan-

dard straight right hand router bits. For best results, router cuts should be kept to a maximum of about 1/8-inch depth. Deeper grooves should be made with a series of cuts. This assures a smooth cutting action and clean straight edges. The motor speed is substantially less than that usually found on routers; therefore, a reduced feed should be employed.

There are two general classifications of router work—straight or irregular. Straight work is done against a fence; irregular work can be cut with a pattern. In either case, the work feed must be against the rotation of the cutter.

Straight Routing. There are two methods of performing straight routing on the radial saw: (1) by moving the material (cutter stationary); and (2) by moving the cutter (material stationary). Most routing operations call for the first method.

In the first method, the cuttinghead is placed in the 90-degree position (the auxiliary motor shaft in a vertical position). Set it on the radial arm for the width of the cut and lock the carriage clamp knob. Then lower the arm by means of the elevating crank to the depth of the cut. Turn on the saw, and keeping the workpiece firmly pressed against the fence, move it slowly past the cutting tool against the rotation of the cutter (Fig. 8-11). Several passes may be necessary to get the desired width and/or depth.

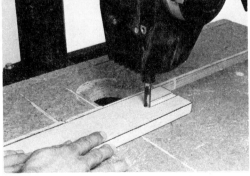

Fig. 8-11: Moving the workpiece past the cutting tool for straight routing.

With the second method, workpiece size is limited by the length of the radial arm. With the router bit in the vertical position and the workpiece against the fence, pull the cuttinghead across the workpiece as you do for crosscutting (Fig. 8-12A). But, keep in mind that cross-grain cuts are a little harder to do, simply because you encounter more resistance. Feed the router bit slowly. Since the travel track serves as a guide, no special jigs are needed when angle routing is done (Fig. 8-12B).

A

B

Fig. 8-12: (A) Straight routing by pulling the cuttinghead across the workpiece; (B) angle routing.

Rabbeting can be done by following either method. Remember, however, to never attempt to take more than about an 1/8-inch cut at a time. (If any degree of force must be applied to accomplish the cut or if excessive chatter is felt, it is safe to assume that you are attempting too deep a cut in one pass.) If a greater depth is desired, lower the arm one turn of the elevating crank at a time. For rabbets wider than the bit, move the cuttinghead forward on the arm so that cuts just overlap each other. Clamp the cuttinghead into position and push the workpiece past the router bit. Continue this movement away from the fence until the required width of the rabbet is obtained.

Circular Routing. Methods of routing grooves in curved or round work are shown in Figs. 8-13 and 8-14. In each case, a block is clamped to the table fence and the cuttinghead is positioned to make the cut where it is needed. If the workpiece has been carefully cut, the waste stock can be utilized as the guide for the work. Be sure to hold the work firmly as you move it around the guide.

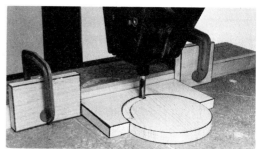

Fig. 8-13: Using the waste stock as a guide for a groove in a circular workpiece.

Fig. 8-14: Another method of routing grooves in a circular workpiece.

Edge Routing. Edge or end grooving is accomplished by placing the workpiece on the boring jig and setting the cutting-head in the horizontal position. The difference between edge boring and routing is that in the latter the material is moved past the bit instead of remaining stationary (Fig. 8-15).

The round-end mortise, previously described as being formed with the boring bits, can also be cut by the edge-routing method to take a round-end tenon. Use the table fence as a guide, with a stop clamped to it to control the length of the slot. Deep cuts should be made in several passes, moving the bit closer to the column after each pass until the full depth of the cut has been obtained.

Fig. 8-15: For edge or end grooving the stock is moved past the router bit.

Pattern Routing. Irregularly shaped stock which cannot be guided against a table fence calls for the use of a routing pattern. In this case the pattern will be a full sized template usually cut from 1/4-inch plywood. The pattern is guided by an auxiliary pin set into the worktable exactly in line with the router bit. The pin must be of the same diameter as the router bit. In use, it projects above the worktable slightly lower than the thickness of the pattern (Fig. 8-16A).

The pattern is fastened to the workpiece with brads and then placed over the guide pin. The bit is set in motion and lowered to the correct depth of cut as the operator holds the pattern. The pattern may then be followed exactly, to produce a similar design on the workpiece (Fig. 8-16B). Before beginning, it is advisable to sketch the pattern outline on the workpiece top to check for accuracy as it is being worked. The guide pin must always be of the same diameter as the router bit and must be centered directly below it.

A major disadvantage of pattern routing is that the pattern is under the work and cannot be seen. This can be overcome by fitting the router bit with a sleeve guide such as shown in Fig. 8-16C.

The pattern is then fastened to the top of the workpiece, and the sleeve, which in this case is a 1/4-inch mortising bushing, turns with the bit and rubs against the pattern outline. Here the pattern should be of hardwood and waxed to minimize friction.

Because the router bit will cut slightly inside the true outline of the pattern because of the sleeve, the required offset should be allowed for when sawing the pattern to shape.

Ornamental Routing. Using a spacer board such as that shown in Fig. 8-17A, it is possible to rout a variety of ornamental moldings. A spacer board is butted against the table fence and the workpiece is fastened to the spacer board. A pin in the table fence engages the saw cuts in the spaced board to guide the repeated router bit cuts (Fig. 8-17B).

BUFFING AND POLISHING

The radial saw can be adapted for various types of finish work. It is suitable for buffing and polishing operations. The tools used for these operations are mounted on the auxiliary motor shaft arbor, using a geared chuck or arbor adaptor. On some radial saws, the buffers are mounted directly on the primary motor shaft, with adaptors, if necessary.

Buffing Operation. The process of restoring a gleaming finish to a pitted or bad-

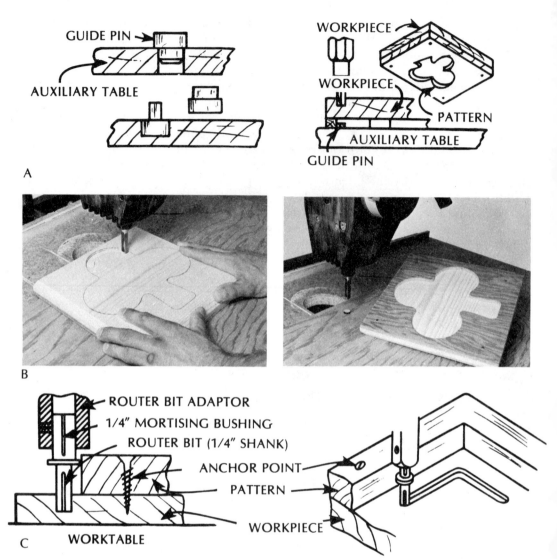

Fig. 8-16: (A) A guide pin used for pattern routing; (B) using a pattern to rout a design on a workpiece; (C) a sleeve guide for pattern routing.

ly tarnished metal surface can be performed easily on your radial saw. To buff a metal surface, mount the cloth buffer on the auxiliary right-hand motor shaft arbor, using a geared chuck or adaptor as required. The motor shaft should be in a horizontal position, as it normally would be for straight crosscutting. If the object is badly pitted, you will have to cut the entire surface down to the level of the deepest pit, using emery composition which comes in a tube or stick.

To charge the buffer, hold the tube or stick to the face of the running buffer and let the heat of friction melt the binder so that it will flow on the wheel. The face of the wheel will turn black when it is well charged. To smooth it down, hold a piece of scrap metal against it with downward, passing strokes. Then, clean the entire surface of the workpiece with the emery-charged buffing wheel.

Chapter 9
THE MOTORIZED MITER BOX

If the radial saw can be classified as a "pull-through" saw, the motorized miter box can be called a "pull-down" saw. The saw blade of the motorized miter box is mounted on an arm which is pulled down into the material to make the cut. Like the radial saw, the motorized miter box is a pretty handy tool to have around the shop. It is ideal for cutting picture frame moldings or other various shaped moldings, and for jobs such as remodeling or general cut-off work. It is designed to cut wood, compositions, plastic, and lightweight soft aluminum extrusions.

As shown in Fig. 9-1, the motorized miter box is a simple tool with few parts and controls. When selecting a machine, however, make certain that it has a brake. A brake lets you stop the blade in seconds, eliminating time-consuming blade coasting while adjusting for the next cut. Also, make sure that the saw blade guard is retractable and offers the operator maximum protection.

The saw blades used with the motorized miter box are generally of the same type that are used with the radial saw (see page 9). The most popular for molding cutting operations, however, is the hollow-ground, novelty combination blade. It gives the smoothest cut of all the blades used on the motorized miter box. Most motorized miter boxes use a 9-inch blade, but be sure to use only saw blades suitable for an operating speed greater than the saw arbor speed.

INSTALLATION
The motorized miter box should be installed in a space that allows for handling workpieces of the maximum anticipated size. Although the motorized miter box can be put on a workbench, it is more readily usable when mounted on a steel or wooden stand of its own. Many steel stands for this tool have accessory casters available which allow for the movement of the motorized miter box to the center of the workshop when it is being used.

The motorized miter box should be unpacked and assembled according to the manufacturer's instructions. The same precautions suggested for the electrical connections of the radial saw found in Chapter 2, apply to the motorized miter box. If an extension cord is necessary, use

Fig. 9-1: The typical motorized miter box.

| Cord | NAMEPLATE AMPERE RATING | | | | | | | | | | | | | | |
Length	0 to 5	6	7	8	9	10	11	12	13	14	15	16	17	18	19	20
25 Ft.	18	18	18	18	18	18	16	16	16	14	14	14	14	14	12	12
50 Ft.	18	18	18	18	18	18	16	16	16	14	14	14	14	14	12	12
75 Ft.	18	18	18	18	18	18	16	16	16	14	14	14	14	14	12	12
100 Ft.	18	18	18	16	16	16	16	16	14	14	14	14	14	14	12	12
125 Ft.	18	18	16	16	16	14	14	14	14	14	14	12	12	12	12	12
150 Ft.	18	16	16	16	14	14	14	14	14	12	12	12	12	12	12	12

Note: Wire sizes shown are AWG (American Wire Gauge) based on a line voltage of 120 and maximum voltage drop (loss) of 10 volts or when cord carries rated current.

only a three-wire cord which has a three-prong grounding-type plug and a three-pole receptacle which accepts the tool's plug. Also, be sure the conductor size is large enough to prevent an excessive voltage drop which will cause loss of power and possible motor damage. A table of recommended extension cord sizes will be found here. For nameplate ampere ratings which are between those given, use the extension cord recommended for the next higher ampere rating.

MOTORIZED MITER BOX ADJUSTMENTS

Adjustment and realignment are necessary to maintain accuracy in any machine—regardless of the care with which the tool is manufactured. Also, moving parts will wear and the abrasive action of dust and dirt adds to this wear. Rough handling during transportation can also throw the machine out of alignment. The following adjustment instructions are general in nature; for specific instructions, check the owner's manual.

Removing "Heeling" in the Saw Cut. Most motorized miter boxes are provided with an adjustment to allow the arbor to be set parallel with the pivot shaft at the rear. The saw blade should be perpendicular to the worktable surface, and also should be at right angles to the pivot shaft. Even

though the blade may be perfectly aligned at 90 degrees to the table, the blade may not be at right angles to the pivot shaft. This condition is called "heeling." To check and adjust, the general procedure is as follows:

1. Clamp a piece of scrap material (about 3 to 3 1/2 inches in height) to the fence, and make a 90 degree cut. Shut off the motor, but do not return the saw blade to the up position.

2. If a condition exists similar to the one shown in Fig. 9-2A, the blade is not at right angles to the pivot shaft and an adjustment is necessary.

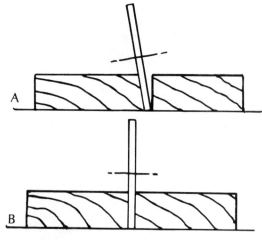

Fig. 9-2: (A) Blade causing "heeling" in the saw cut; (B) proper position of the blade as it makes a straight crosscut.

Fig. 9-3: Screws for adjusting the blade square to the pivot shaft.

3. **Disconnect the machine from the power circuit.** Then remove the blade guard. Loosen the three screws (A) (Fig. 9-3), and shift the entire cuttinghead until the blade is at right angles to the pivot shaft. Tighten the three screws (A), and re-check until you are certain the saw blade is not "heeling" and is entering the work as shown in Fig. 9-2B.

Leveling the Table. Because of the saw kerf, the worktable may tend to sag in the center. To prevent this, a flat head screw, slotted at both ends, is provided in the base. To level the table, place a straight edge across the worktable. If an adjust-

Fig. 9-4: Leveling the table.

ment is necessary, tighten or loosen the screw (A) (Fig. 9-4), until the flat head on the other end of the screw comes into contact with the bottom of the worktable when the table is level.

Adjusting the Table Square with the Fence and Blade. It is important that the worktable is square with the fence and blade. The general procedure to do this is as follows:

1. Place a square on the table with one end of the square against the fence, as shown in Fig. 9-5.

2. If an adjustment to the table is necessary, tighten or loosen the screws (A), until

Fig. 9-5: Adjusting the table square with the fence.

the table is square with the fence. Note: The table is mounted on four resilient pads.

3. Repeat this adjustment on the opposite end of the table.

4. Place the square against the blade and table as shown in Fig. 9-6.

5. If an adjustment is necessary, tighten or loosen the screws (A), until the table is square with the blade.

Operating the Control Arm. Most motorized miter boxes will cut any angle from 90 degrees to 45 degrees right or left. Loosen the arm lock knob (A) (Fig. 9-7), and move the control arm (B) to the desired angle, and tighten the arm lock knob (A).

Many machines also contain positive stops at 90 and 45 degrees, right and left.

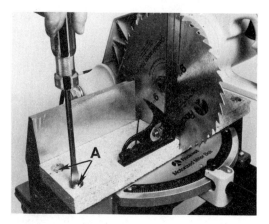

Fig. 9-6: Adjusting the table square with the blade.

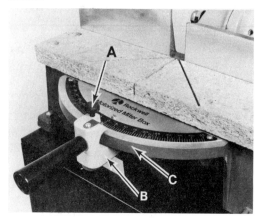

Fig. 9-7: Operating the control arm.

Simply loosen the lock knob (A) and move the control arm until the spring-loaded positive stop engages into the indent located directly underneath the ledge (C). Then tighten the arm lock knob (A).

Adjusting the 90-degree Positive Stop. To check and adjust the 90-degree positive stop in most machines, proceed as follows:

1. Loosen the arm lock knob (A) (Fig. 9-7), and move the arm (B) to the center of the scale until the spring-loaded positive stop engages into the factory pre-drilled indent, located underneath the ledge (C). Then tighten the arm lock knob (A).

2. Make a cut on a piece of scrapboard and check with a square to see if the piece of wood was cut at 90 degrees (Fig. 9-8).

3. If an adjustment is necessary, snug-up the arm lock knob (A) and loosen the two screws (B) (Fig. 9-9), one-half to one turn. Then tap the arm (C) to the right or left as necessary, and tighten the two screws (B).

4. Make another test cut, and if further adjustment is necessary, repeat the above instructions.

5. When you are certain the cut is at 90 degrees, adjust the pointer to the 0 degree mark on the scale.

6. The positive stops at 45 degrees right and 45 degrees left are factory set and should require no further adjustment.

Adjusting the Downward Travel of the Saw Blade. The downward travel of the saw blade can generally be limited to prevent

Fig. 9-8: Checking a scrapboard cut on the motorized miter box for squareness.

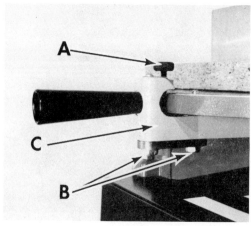

Fig. 9-9: Adjusting the 90-degree positive stop.

the saw blade from cutting too far into the table. With most motorized miter boxes, this adjustment is made by loosening locknut (A) Fig. 9-10, and turning the adjusting screw (B) in or out to the desired position.

Adjusting the Spring Tension of the Overarm. The overarm is adjusted at the factory so that it returns to the up position and remains there. If it ever becomes necessary to re-adjust the spring tension of the overarm, the general procedure is: loosen the locknut (D) Fig. 9-10, and tighten or loosen the adjusting nut (C) until the correct spring tension of the overarm is obtained. Then tighten the locknut (D).

Replacing the Saw Blade. To remove the saw blade from the motorized miter box,

Fig. 9-10: Adjusting the downward travel of the saw blade.

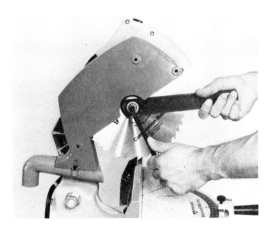

Fig. 9-11: Using two special wrenches to remove the saw blade from the arbor shaft.

proceed as follows:

1. **Disconnect the machine from the power source.**

2. Remove the saw blade guard.

3. Using the two special wrenches supplied with the machine, loosen the arbor nut with one wrench while holding the arbor shaft steady with the other wrench (Fig. 9-11). Keep in mind that the arbor nut has a left hand thread.

4. Remove the arbor nut and slide the blade off the saw arbor. Replace with the new blade, making sure that the teeth of the saw blade face down at the front. Tighten the arbor nut, reversing the procedure shown in Fig. 9-11.

5. Replace the saw blade guard and plug the machine into the power source.

Starting and Stopping the Machine. To start the motorized miter box, depress the switch trigger. To stop the machine, release the switch trigger.

Most motorized miter boxes are equipped with a blade brake. As soon as the cut is completed, release the switch trigger (A) and press down on the brake button B, as shown in Fig. 9-12. Always, apply the brake immediately, to stop the saw blade when the switch is released. Remember that a coasting blade can be dangerous.

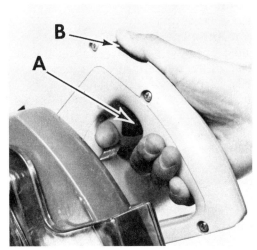

Fig. 9-12: (A) The switch trigger; (B) the brake button.

MAINTENANCE TIPS

Although the motorized miter box requires little maintenance, the following checks should be made on occasion to make sure problems do not arise:

1. Check all nuts, bolts, and screws for tightness.

2. Check the belt to make certain it is in good condition. Most motorized miter boxes have toothed or cogged belts. If it becomes necessary to replace the belt, follow the manufacturer's instructions given in the owner's manual.

3. Make sure the blade guard operates properly.

4. Regular oil or grease is *not* recommended for the lubrication of the moving parts of this tool. Use one of the available silicone products when it is necessary to lubricate the moving parts.

5. Check the brushes at regular intervals. Brush life, of course, varies, depending upon the load on the motor. For a new machine or after a new set of brushes has been installed, check the brushes after the first 50 hours of use. Once the first check is made, examine them after about 10 hours of use until such time that a replacement is necessary. When the carbon on either brush is worn to 3/16 inch in length, or if either spring or shunt wire is burned or damaged in any way, replace both brushes. The brush holders are located on the end of the motor opposite each other. If the brushes are found serviceable after removing, reinstall them in the same position they were in before being removed (Fig. 9-13). *Note:* Before inspecting the brushes, **disconnect the machine from the power source.**

6. Keep all working parts free from sawdust and other substances that might have an abrasive effect on the parts. Also, clean out the sawdust from underneath the worktable at regular intervals.

7. Blade teeth tend to become clogged with sawdust and resin; this causes dragging during the cut. Clean frequently,

Fig. 9-13: *Inspecting the motor brushes on the motorized miter box.*

using a resin solvent when necessary, and apply a light coating of rust preventative. **Note: When using solvents, be sure the area is adequately ventilated.**

8. Never use solvents to clean plastic parts. Solvents could possibly dissolve or otherwise damage the plastic. Only a soft damp cloth should be used to clean plastic parts.

9. Keep the worktable in good condition. When replacing the table becomes necessary, a new one may be purchased or you may construct a new table out of a suitable material. The dimensions given in Fig. 9-14 may be varied to fit your machine.

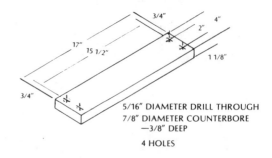

Fig. 9-14: *Average dimensions for a replacement table.*

TROUBLESHOOTING GUIDE

In spite of how well a motorized miter box is maintained, problems do come along. The following troubleshooting guide will help you solve the more common problems:

Trouble: *Tool will not start.*

Probable Cause	Remedy
1. Saw not plugged in.	1. Plug in saw.
2. Fuse blown or circuit breaker tripped.	2. Replace fuse or reset circuit breaker.
3. Cord damaged.	3. Have cord replaced.

Trouble: *Tool makes unsatisfactory cuts.*

Probable Cause	Remedy
1. Dull blade.	1. Replace blade.
2. Blade mounted backwards.	2. Turn blade around.
3. Gum or pitch on blade.	3. Remove blade and clean with turpentine and coarse steel wool.
4. Incorrect blade for work being done.	4. Change the blade.

Trouble: *Blade does not come up to speed.*

Probable Cause	Remedy
1. Extension cord too light or too long.	1. Replace with adequate size cord.
2. Low supply voltage.	2. Contact your electric company.

Trouble: *Machine vibrates excessively.*

Probable Cause	Remedy
1. Saw not mounted securely to stand or work bench.	1. Tighten all mounting hardware.
2. Stand or bench on uneven floor.	2. Reposition on flat level surface. Fasten to floor if necessary.
3. Damaged saw blade.	3. Replace blade.

Trouble: *Does not make accurate 45 and 90 degree cuts.*

Probable Cause	Remedy
1. Positive stop not adjusted correctly.	1. Check and adjust positive stop.
2. Blade is "heeling."	2. Check and adjust cuttinghead.
3. Table not square with fence.	3. Check and adjust table.

Trouble: *Material pinches blade.*

Probable Cause	Remedy
1. Cutting bowed material in wrong position.	1. Position bowed material as shown on page 118.
2. Sag in table.	2. Level table.

Trouble: *Saw blade cuts too deeply into worktable.*

Probable Cause	Remedy
1. Adjustable stop not set correctly.	1. Check and adjust stop screw.

Trouble: *Saw blade does not return to up position.*

Probable Cause	Remedy
1. Spring tension out of adjustment.	1. Adjust return spring tension.

MOTORIZED MITER BOX SAFETY

Many of the safety tips for the radial saw, given in Chapter 2, apply to the motorized miter box, as well. But, here are some additional tips to keep in mind when operating this tool:

1. Be sure the blade is sharp, free cutting and free from vibration.

2. Use the saw blade guard. **Never operate the machine with the guard removed.**

3. Wear safety goggles or a face shield whenever operating the motorized miter box.

4. Allow the motor to come up to full speed before starting to cut.

5. Always hold the work firmly against the fence. When necessary, employ a mechanical holding device or a homemade support. Never hand-hold a workpiece that is too small to be firmly grasped, while keeping your fingers at least 3 inches from the cutting path of the blade.

6. Release the trigger switch before applying the brake.

7. Use the brake to bring the blade to a stop before reaching out to pick up a workpiece, a piece of scrap, or anything else which is in or near the cutting path of the blade. Make sure the motorized miter box has come to a complete stop before leaving the machine unattended.

OPERATION OF THE MOTORIZED MITER BOX

Baseboards and similar moldings, even 2 x 4s, can be easily crosscut (Fig. 9-15A) or miter angle cut (Fig. 9-15B) by placing the stock flat on the worktable against the fence. The motorized miter box can be set at any angle from 45 to 90 degrees, left or right. If you wish to cut a bevel angle (the range is again 45 to 90 degrees), the workpiece is placed on edge against the fence as illustrated in Fig. 9-16. But, regardless of the sawing operation, it is very important that the workpiece be well-supported. Never attempt to hand-hold work that causes your fingers to be 3 inches or less from the blade. Also, do not try to balance

A

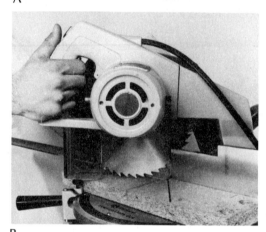

B

Fig. 9-15: Making (A) a crosscut, and (B) a miter angle cut on the motorized miter box.

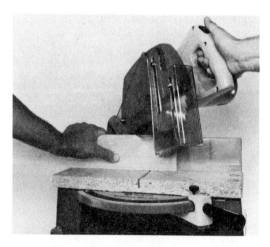

Fig. 9-16: Cutting a bevel angle.

an uneven workpiece by hand.

There are some operations of the motorized miter box that require special holding setups. For instance, Fig. 9-17 illustrates a filler block that can easily be constructed for use in cutting bevel miters. The face of the filler block is shown at 45 degrees to the fence and table. If a different work angle tilt is desired, simply vary the angle of the filler block face accordingly. That is, the angle at the bottom of the filler block will determine the bevel angle of the cut; the machine's control setting will determine the miter angle.

Although in Fig. 9-17 the face of the filler block is shown to be 3 5/8 inches wide, this dimension will vary depending on the workpiece being cut. To prevent the work from creeping, fasten the filler blocks to the fence by drilling two holes in each side of the metal fence and secure the blocks to the fence with wood screws from the rear.

Figures 9-18 and 9-19 illustrate two different methods that can be used when cutting crown moldings. The majority of crown moldings have contact surfaces at 52 and 38 degrees respectively to the rear surface of the molding. These angles must be utilized when jointing the face of the filler block. For crown moldings with different angles, appropriate filler blocks can be produced.

Figure 9-18 shows the filler block mounted to the fence with the face of the filler block extending outward from the top of the fence and down to the surface of the table. When the filler block is positioned in this manner, the crown molding must be placed on the table upside down. Figure 9-19 shows the filler block reversed, whereby the face extends inward toward the fence from top to bottom. When the crown molding is positioned in this manner, it is placed on the table in the same position as it would be when nailed between the ceiling and wall.

The filler blocks shown in both Figs. 9-18 and 9-19 are fastened to the fence by drill-

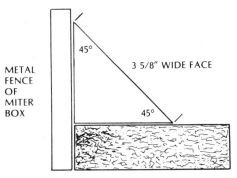

Fig. 9-17: A filler block for use in cutting bevel miters.

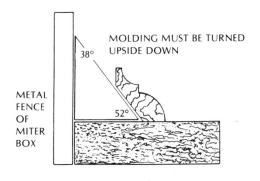

Fig. 9-18: Filler block for cutting crown molding, with the block extending outward from the top of the fence.

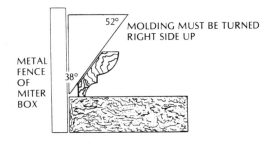

Fig. 9-19: Filler block for cutting crown molding with the face extending inward toward the fence from top to bottom.

ing two holes in each side of the fence and securing the blocks to the fence with round head wood screws from the rear.

When 45 degree right hand miters are

required for baseboards that are between 3 and 3 5/8 inches in height, three helpful hints that will make the task easier, are as follows.

1. Instead of cutting the angle 45 degrees to the right, simply flop the work over, so that the face is against the fence, and cut a 45 degree angle to the left as shown in Fig. 9-20.

2. Make a 90 degree cut in the work about 1/4 inch to the right of where you wish to make the 45 degree right angle cut. The 45 degree right angle cut can then be made as shown in Fig. 9-21.

Fig. 9-20: A 45-degree right-hand miter can be cut by flopping the workpiece over and cutting a 45-degree angle to the left.

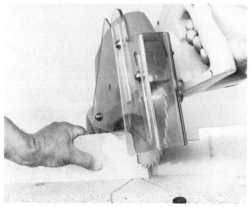

Fig. 9-21: Cutting a 45-degree right-hand miter in baseboard molding.

3. Construct two spacing blocks by following the dimensions given in Fig. 9-22A. The blocks can be fastened to the table by drilling and counterboring holes through the blocks and fastening the blocks to the table with wood screws, or two holes can be drilled on each side of the fence and the blocks can be secured to the fence with round head wood screws from the rear.

When applying ceiling molding, it is not necessary to miter all four corners. Measure the longest side of the ceiling and cut a length of molding about 1/16th of an inch longer than required (you may have to cut two or more lengths for an extra long ceiling). Each end of the molding should be cut square, not mitered. Bow the molding so it can be snapped into place and secure it with brads or finishing nails. Drive the nails a little below the surface with a nail set and fill with wood putty. Do the same for the molding for the opposite side of the room. The molding for the two remaining short sides of the room are then "coped" to fit. A coped joint has an important advantage over a mitered joint because it can be made to fit even when the corner is somewhat out of square.

There are two basic ways to make a coped joint. The first method is to make a miter cut on the molding and then cut away the excess wood using the edge of the miter cut as a guide. A coping saw is used for this operation—which is why it is called a coped joint. However, instead of cutting at an exact angle to the face of the molding, the saw should be eased slightly backward so that the back of the molding is somewhat

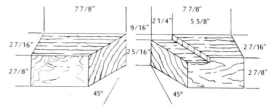

Fig. 9-22: Dimensions for spacing blocks for making miter cuts.

shorter than the front (Fig. 9-23A). This is done for the sake of clearance. This type of coped joint is always used when the back of the molding does not have a plain, flat surface—which is always the case with crown molding used for ceiling work.

The second method of making a coped joint is somewhat easier than the first. However, it can only be used with molding that has a flat surface on the back. Cut a short piece of molding, about 2 or 3 inches long, and trace its outline on the back of the molding you want to cope. Hold it true and perpendicular, and use a sharp pencil to make the outline. Next, tape the front to avoid splintering as you will be cutting from the back, and place the molding in a vise. Use the coping saw, again cutting at a slight backward angle for clearance. Cut through the molding, following the pencil line on the back (Fig. 9-23B). In either case, the coped molding will fit perfectly to the molding to which it has been coped (Fig. 9-23C).

A coped joint can only be used in an interior corner, while a mitered joint can be used for both interior and exterior corners. Here are a few points to remember when making mitered and coped joints.

1. To get an accurate measurement of the length of molding required for an exterior miter, nick the molding with a sharp knife held flat against the intersecting wall surface. Remember, this mark represents the short side of the miter. Always make allowance for waste and the thickness of the saw cut.

2. To get the exact length for a long piece of molding where it is difficult to use a steel tape and a six-foot folding rule is too short, overlap two pieces of straight stiff molding. To get the correct length required, mark with a sharp pencil the end of one piece where the overlap ends.

3. Always place the molding in the motorized miter box in the position it will occupy on the floor or ceiling.

4. If possible, always cut the molding with the good side facing the saw blade. Also, use a hollow ground miter saw blade

A

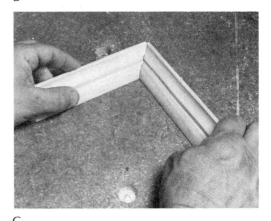

B

C

Fig. 9-23: (A) Instead of cutting at an exact angle to the face of the molding, the blade is eased slightly backward so that the back of the molding is shorter than the front; (B) cutting through molding by following a pencil line on the back for making a coped joint; (C) fitting coped molding.

(4 cutting teeth—1 raker tooth) for cutting molding.

5. Hold the molding firmly while cutting it. If necessary, use a C-clamp or nail it on the waste side to the worktable or auxiliary fence of the motorized miter box. *Note:* Certain moldings will tend to creep when they are mitered. To eliminate this condition, glue several strips of sandpaper to the fence.

6. When nailing the molding in place, stagger the nails, one near the top and another nail near the bottom. This will prevent unsightly gaps at the top and bottom. Always countersink the nailheads with a nail set and fill the holes with wood putty.

When cutting flat pieces, it is important to check to see if the stock is bowed. If it is, make sure the work is positioned with the convex side against the fence as shown in Fig. 9-24A. If the workpiece is positioned with the concave side against the fence as shown in Fig. 9-24B, it will pinch the blade near the completion of the cut.

PICTURE FRAME CUTTING

One of the major uses of the motorized miter box in the home shop is to cut picture frames. The moldings for the frames can frequently be made on a radial saw equipped with a molding cutterhead (see Chapter 6). Molding can also be purchased ready-made.

Figure 9-25 illustrates how to measure the sizes of molding needed to make a

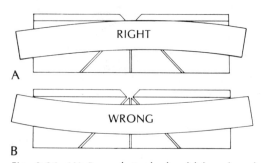

Fig. 9-24: (A) Bowed stock should be placed with the convex side against the fence; (B) the stock will pinch the blade if the concave side is against the fence.

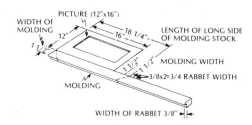

Fig. 9-25: Method of measuring molding for making a picture frame.

frame. On the outside of the molding stock, lay out for the length of the picture, and add to that, twice the width of the molding, minus twice the width of the rabbet. Do the same with the width of the picture. Add about 1/16 inch to both lengths of molding so that the glass and picture will fit loosely in the finished frame. The example shown in Fig. 9-25 is worked out as follows:

Picture Length 16 inches	16"
Molding Width 1 1/2 inches X 2 = 3 inches	+3"
	19"
Rabbet Width 3/8 inch X 2 = 3/4 inch	− 3/4"
	18 1/4"
Plus 1/16 inch for clearance	+ 1/16"
Length of Long Side of Frame Molding	18 5/16"
Picture Width 12 inches	12"
Molding Width 1 1/2 inches X 2 = 3 inches	+3"
	15"
Rabbet Width 3/8 inch X 2 = 3/4 inch	− 3/4"
	14 1/4"
Plus 1/16 inch for clearance	+ 1/16"
Length of Short Side of Frame Molding	14 5/16"

Since most picture-frame moldings have a flat back, place the workpiece face up on the tool's worktable and miter cut the ends, right and left, respectively. When a shadow-box effect is desired, use the filler block shown in Fig. 9-17, and make bevel cuts as described previously.

CUTTING ALUMINUM AND PLASTIC

Cutting soft aluminum extrusions and bar stock can be accomplished with a motorized miter box in the same way as similar wooden sections. But when positioning such material, be sure the blade is cutting through the smallest cross section (Fig. 9-

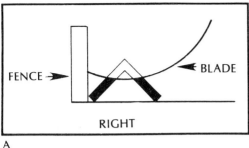

A

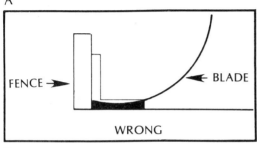

B

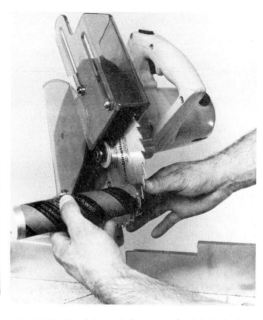

Fig. 9-26: (A) Be sure to cut aluminum extrusions through the smallest cross section; (B) the wrong way to position aluminum for cutting.

Fig. 9-27: Applying stick wax to the blade before cutting aluminum. Be sure the power is disconnected before starting this operation.

26A). Figure 9-26B illustrates the wrong way to cut aluminum angles.

When cutting aluminum with the motorized miter box, be sure to apply a stick wax to the blade (Fig. 9-27) before each cut. This is done to provide proper lubrication and to keep chips from adhering to the blade. Stick wax for this purpose is available at most industrial mill supply houses.

Plastic tubing, pipe, and extrusions can be cut with a motorized miter box in the same manner as similar wood workpieces.

INCH/MILLIMETER CONVERSIONS

INCHES TO MILLIMETERS Multiply inches by 25.4				MILLIMETERS TO INCHES Multiply millimeters by 0.03937	
INCHES	**MILLIMETERS**	**INCHES**	**MILLIMETERS**	**MILLIMETERS**	**INCHES**
.001	.025	17/32	13.4938	.001	.00004
.01	.254	35/64	13.8906	.01	.00039
1/64	.3969	9/16	14.2875	.02	.00079
.02	.508	37/64	14.6844	.03	.00118
.03	.762	19/32	15.0812	.04	.00157
1/32	.7938	.6	15.24	.05	.00196
.04	1.016	39/64	15.4781	.06	.00236
3/64	1.191	5/8	15.875	.07	.00276
.05	1.27	41/64	16.2719	.08	.00315
.06	1.524	21/32	16.6688	.09	.00354
1/16	1.5875	43/64	17.0656	.1	.00394
.07	1.778	11/16	17.4625	.2	.00787
5/64	1.9844	.7	17.78	.3	.01181
.08	2.032	45/64	17.8594	.4	.01575
.09	2.286	23/32	18.2562	.5	.01969
3/32	2.3812	47/64	18.6531	.6	.02362
.1	2.54	3/4	19.050	.7	.02756
7/64	2.7781	49/64	19.4469	.8	.0315
1/8	3.175	25/32	19.8438	.9	.03543
9/64	3.5719	51/64	20.2406	1.0	.03937
5/32	3.9688	.8	20.32	2.0	.07874
11/64	4.3656	13/16	20.6375	3.0	.11811
3/16	4.7625	53/64	21.0344	4.0	.15748
.2	5.08	27/32	21.4312	5.0	.19685
13/64	5.1594	55/64	21.8281	6.0	.23622
7/32	5.5562	7/8	22.225	7.0	.27559
15/64	5.9531	57/64	22.6219	8.0	.31496
1/4	6.35	.9	22.86	9.0	.35433
17/64	6.7469	29/32	23.0188	1 CM	.3937
9/32	7.1438	59/64	23.4156	2 CM	.7874
19/64	7.5406	15/16	23.8125	3 CM	1.1811
.3	7.62	61/64	24.2094	4 CM	1.5748
5/16	7.9375	31/32	24.6062	5 CM	1.9685
21/64	8.3344	63/64	25.0031	6 CM	2.3622
11/32	8.7312	1.0	25.4	7 CM	2.7559
23/64	9.1281	2.0	50.8	8 CM	3.1496
3/8	9.525	3.0	76.2	9 CM	3.5433
25/64	9.9219	4.0	101.6	1 DM	3.937
.4	10.16	5.0	127.0	2 DM	7.874
13/32	10.3188	6.0	152.4	3 DM	11.811
27/64	10.7156	7.0	177.8	4 DM	1 Ft., 3.748
7/16	11.1125	8.0	203.2		
29/64	11.5094	9.0	228.6	**ABBREVIATIONS**	
15/32	11.9062	10.0	254.0	MM-Millimeter(1/1000)	
31/64	12.3031	11.0	279.4	CM-Centimeter(1/100)	
1/2	12.7	1 Ft.	304.8	DM-Decimeter(1/10)	
33/64	13.0969				

Index